Get Off
Your Rocker

Before You
Go Off
Your Rocker

Get Off Your Rocker

Before You Go Off Your Rocker

A Guide to Retirement

Barry M. Bograd

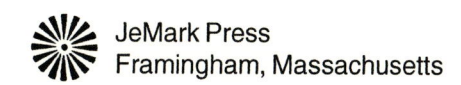
JeMark Press
Framingham, Massachusetts

This book is intended to provide reliable, competent information on this subject. It is sold with the explicit understanding that the publisher and author are not engaged in rendering advice of a professional, legal or emotional nature.

If legal or other expert advice is needed and/or required, services of professionals should be procured. Laws and practices may vary from state to state. The publisher and author specifically disclaim any liability that is incurred from the application or use of this book.

Published by

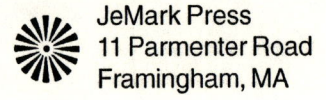 JeMark Press
11 Parmenter Road
Framingham, MA

ISBN 0-9768812-0-9

Visit our website at www.getoffyourrocker.com

Printed in the United States of America

Cover and Book Design by Pauline E. Kelly

Praise for

Get Off Your Rocker
Before You Go Off Your Rocker

Knowing Barry all my life as a classmate, teammate and friend, he always had good ideas so it's no surprise to me that his success continues through retirement with this terrific book.

Joe DeNucci, Massachusetts State Auditor
Former World Middleweight Contender

This interesting book provides lots of helpful financial tips that will help you make the most of your retirement.

Jonathan Pond, host of numerous public television specials,
Financial Commentator for CNN,
and author of 13 books on Personal Financial Planning

This is a must-read book for anyone who is retired, is about to retire, wants to retire, or will some day. Having known Barry for going on 50 years, I am not surprised that he is once again ahead of the curve. This work is full of fascinating profiles who have moved into their retirement, along with invaluable tips to help you with your transition. Congratulations on a terrific book that belongs on everyone's shelf.

Paul Guzzi, President and CEO, Greater Boston Chamber of Commerce
Former Secretary of State

I've been waiting for years for a book like this to come out. For those of us on the verge of retirement there really aren't many options when it comes to assessing our prospects. Barry Bograd has answered loads of questions that I've begun to think seriously about while contemplating the next phase of my life. He truly has a rare insight into the concerns of the rapidly growing retirement population.

Bob Gatti, President and Founder, Gatti & Associates

Barry has struck a chord for the individual recently retired or retiring. Case histories are a wonderful way to experience other people's choices. Doing your homework about finances, healthcare, outside activities, etc., all add up to success for you, and success for Barry's book.

Ricky (Ruth Ann) Moriarty, Former Executive Director,
Operation A.B.L.E., Boston, MA

Most people prepare for their life's work but most people don't prepare for retirement. Barry Bograd's insightful and illuminating book will be an asset for anyone preparing to retire.

Tom Concannon
Former Mayor of Newton, Massachusetts

To

my wonderful wife of 40 years, Elaine

To our devoted sons and their families,
who have always
been an inspiration to me:

Jeff, Karen, Nicholas, Emma,
and Harrison

Mark, Brooke, and Samantha

To my parents, Ida and Phil, who have always
been there for me

Thank you for your continuous love and
support throughout the years.

Contents

Acknowledgements

Writing a book is a daunting experience, especially for the uninitiated. There is so much more to it than just putting pen to paper. The ideas are one thing, but the process is a different story. If it's your first time, then you really need a coach to take you through the steps. I was indeed fortunate to hook up with a woman who has written and published three successful books. Martha R. A. Fields and I go back several years together in the field of Human Resources. We served together on the Bentley College Human Resources Advisory Board.

I had written articles in the past, but never anything as challenging as an entire book. There is no question that this work could not have been accomplished without the encouragement of Ms. Fields and her right hand person, Jessie Shea. Their gentle prodding and critiquing helped create what you hopefully will find entertaining and educational. They both have my debt of gratitude, admiration, and heartfelt thanks for showing me the way.

Being an idea guy, grammar and punctuation sometimes gets in my way. Editor Pauline Kelly deserves lots of kudos for a magnificent editing job. She followed it up with the layout and designed the striking cover. A great big thank you for all her excellent and hard work.

This book could not have become a reality without the openness and honest sharing by the wonderful people who are profiled. They took time out from their busy schedules to share their stories with all of us. As you will see, there is a great deal of candor within these pages. They left nothing on the table; they covered it all – the good and the bad.

To my friends who have supported me in all my ventures throughout the years, I can never thank them enough. To the late Jack Erdlen and George Rossi, to Bob Gatti, Nancy Rogoff, Jack Fusco, Lou Rubino, Harry Sobel, Tom Concannon, Marty Schwartz, Sylvia Lewis, Bob Merusi, and Dick Quigley – thank you for your generous support and for always being in my corner.

And finally to my family. I am truly blessed to have a soulmate who shares all of my world, my wife of 40 years, Elaine. My sons and their families have been a constant source of inspiration. To Jeff, his wife, Karen, and our grandchildren, Nicholas, age nine, Emma, age five, and Harrison, age one, and to Mark, his wife, Brooke, our granddaughter Samantha, 20 months old – great big hugs and kisses and thank yous.

When you reach 65 years of age and you are still lucky enough to have both of your parents alive and well, it is truly a blessing. My parents Ida, and Phil, share in all our joys and joyous occasions. Since I'm an only child, it's been the three of us for all these years. I could never repay them for all of their encouragement.

Thank you, the reader, for thinking enough about this subject and this message to buy our book. We do hope you enjoy it.

Barry M. Bograd

Introduction

Couldn't wait to retire. I counted down the years, the months, and finally the days. The big day came 90 days ago. I was free at last! It was as if the weight of the world had been lifted off my shoulders.

Let me recount what it's been like: I slept late, played a lot of golf, read a couple of good books, and took a fabulous cruise to the Caribbean. Okay, I'm done with that. Like the Peggy Lee song says, "Is That All There Is?" What's next? I have hopefully 20-30 good years left. Am I going to sit in my easy chair, contemplate life, and look at the four walls? I don't think so! There is only so much *Oprah, Dr. Phil* and *Court TV* that I can take. I wonder what others in my situation are doing? How can I fill my time? What's out there for me to do?

And, will inflation and low interest rates kill my retirement nest egg? I already had to put retirement off for a couple of years due to that damn stock market. Who would have thought that it would tank for three-plus years? Should I work part-time, either for income, or more importantly, for my sanity? I'm really confused. Maybe I wasn't ready and prepared for retirement. I'm a little nervous, and frankly, between you and me, kind of scared. Where do I go from here? Someone give me some advice. Give me some options. *Help!*

Sound familiar? If it does, you're not the Lone Ranger. There are so many of us with the same conundrums, that I decided to write a book about the challenges of retirement.

Over the next several chapters you will read about people who have re-written the stereotypic norm of retirement. We could even call what some people do as "free-hirement" or "re-hirement." There is no right or wrong answer to the question, "What do I do next?" It's always in the eye of the beholder.

In this book, we will look at ten profiles of people who have moved from their work life to the "next phase." The next phase is as diversified as the people themselves. Reading this book should give you good ideas and a head start on what is out there to do. In addition to individual profiles, you will find helpful tips about preparing financially, staying healthy, and things to do to remain sane during retirement. Don't be pressured into doing things you don't want to do. You've worked hard all your life. There is more to do. Yes, you are retiring from one phase, but that doesn't necessarily mean you have to hang up your cleats. There are a myriad of activities to keep you interested, vibrant, and healthy that can be rewarding to you and to those with whom you interface.

Sit back, relax and join us on a journey to the next phase of your life. So let's help you *Get Off Your Rocker Before You Go Off Your Rocker*. Thanks for coming along for the ride.

Part I

Yesterday,
Today,
and
Tomorrow

The Stories
of Our Lives

1

Like the Energizer Bunny, He Keeps on Going

You know what is tough? Interviewing yourself. But when I conceived of writing a book of this nature, my own world came into play. My biggest fear was that my retirement would be spent on my leather chair staring at the four walls, and I was bound and determined not to let that happen. So hopefully, you the reader, will not think it is too brazen of me to look into the mirror and share with you how this 65 year-old retiree got to where he is today.

I have always been fascinated with the question, "How did you get to be who you are?" I once hosted a cable television show with that title, and I interviewed people with diverse backgrounds and occupations. The local school department thought the shows were so informative, they used them as training vehicles in their career services module. But more about that later.

Barry Bograd (me) is the product of a very atypical childhood, which led to creating the persona I possess today. I was born in Boston in 1940. At that time, my folks were living in rural New Hampshire, down the road from the University of New Hampshire, and I spent the first four years of my life living on a quiet street in a quiet, small town USA, in a small matchbox type of house attached to three others (like "row houses"). My grandparents, aunts, uncles, and cousins all lived there, in a classic 1940s, WWII setting.

My family was in the shoe business (workers not owners), and my dad worked in the factory by day and played the trumpet at night. Even though we were in the middle of a great World War, we were at peace with ourselves in this tranquil setting. And so my early values were formed by being around our extended family every day.

When I reached four years-old, a crescendo of culture shock descended upon me. My dad had the great opportunity to play trumpet in Leonard Bernstein's first Broadway show, *On the Town*, starring Nancy Walker, and we moved from the backwoods of Newmarket, New Hampshire to Broadway in one fell swoop. We moved to Sunnyside, Long Island – just over the Tri-Borough Bridge – and overnight my life changed forever.

The next two years infused me with influences that would affect who I was going to be the rest of my life. My dad went on the road with the show, and we traveled cross-country on trains to Hollywood where he would make Big Band movies. I was the only child traveling with the band, so my playmates were all adults. The trains did not have enough seats, so we were forced to sit on luggage for many of the miles. At stops, I would get off the train with the soldiers, and they would buy candy for me. In return, I would sing and dance and entertain them. One time they forgot to get me back on the train and we almost were left at the station!

I had a shock of curly hair, a big smile, and I loved to entertain. I was told that Nancy Sinatra (who sang the hit song, *These Boots Were Made for Walking*) and I were an item in Hollywood, playing together while our fathers were performing. We lived close to the intersection of Hollywood and Vine in 1945 – Wow! I still tease my folks, who are 92 and 91 years-old today and still going strong, saying, "Why didn't you let me stay in Hollywood and get into show business? You'd never know who I'd be today!"

However, after a while, my mother, a proper Bostonian, had enough of that life, and back to New York we came, although not for long. My dad hooked up with many of the well-known bands of that era – Frankie Carle, George Paxton, and Jerry Wald, just to name a few.

Meanwhile the precocious Barry was now a five year-old and it was time for kindergarten…oops, he rebelled and kicked the teacher at orientation. The teachers said he was not quite ready for school and to try again next year. We must remember that his frame of reference was adult musicians, not five year-olds. My mother tried a parochial day school, but I ran away through the New York traffic back to our apartment, #5J, at 4142 42nd Street.

I had fun standing on my tricycle and changing the stoplights when they left the box open. Oh yeah – I hate eggs! When they served hard-boiled eggs for lunch at the "Yeshiva," in my pocket they would go. Did you ever try to get dried egg out of a corduroy pants pocket at the end of the day?

Finally, at age six, I attempted the school routine again. This time it worked. The kid was ready. But after a few weeks, I came home with a new word – "kirf." My Boston-bred mother asked, "What?" I repeated the word, and she told me to spell it. I said, "C-A-L-F – kirf." She fumed at my father, "That's it, Phil. My kid is not going to grow up talking like this – we're going back to Boston."

Within weeks my father and grandfather, without their wives, bought a two-family home in Newtonville, Massachusetts, and once again, my life changed forever. Who knows who I would have become if, one, we had stayed in Hollywood, or two, we had stayed in New

York, or three, we never left New Hampshire? However, we did, and the next section will explore why I was the youngest kid in the Newton High School Class of 1957.

Coming to Newtonville at age six was probably the best thing that could have happened to me. Having only three months of formal schooling in the first grade, the natural move would have been to place me in the first grade in Newtonville. However, after extensive testing and interviews, the administration decided I would be bored in the first grade, and therefore my Newton school career began as a six and one-half year-old in grade two. And that is why I was the youngest kid in the class when I graduated Newton High School at age 17. I would not recommend this, and in retrospect I'm sure that life leading up to graduation was harder than it had to be.

My strong points were music (I played the clarinet and sax), performing (acting and singing), and sports. I was a "B/C" student who often got by using my personality. I majored in extra-curricula activities that would hold me in good stead for the rest of my life.

I wanted to go to college away from home, but it was not to be. Boston University was not a fun place if you were a commuter. At least not for me. The academics were hard and the social life was not great. My only solace was that I fell in love with R.O.T.C. and intramural sports. Living at home with no car available was very difficult, and not how I had envisioned college life.

I vowed that if I ever had children they would never commute to college. I can honestly say that for me the only redeeming value of going to Boston University was that I received my degree in Psychology in 1961, and at the same time was commissioned a Second Lieutenant in the U.S. Army Transportation Corp. I was in the top 10 percent of the class and was offered a Regular Army commission (as in West Point or the Citadel), but opted to take the reserve commission which committed me for two years instead of three, with the possibility of a career.

When I finally went on active duty in April 1962, ten months after my graduation, a whole new world opened up for me. It was what I thought college life would be like. I went to Ft. Eustis, Virginia (Transportation School) for nine weeks and then to Ludwigsburg (Stuttgart) Germany for two years. I met my fiancée the night before leaving for Germany, and began a long distance relationship that lasted a year and one-quarter and resulted in an engagement and disengagement during my tour of duty overseas. It was nobody's fault – just too much too quick. It's too long a story to tell, but very atypical for this very typical boy.

The military was great, and two of the most interesting years of my life. During this time, I was a Platoon Leader, an Executive Officer, and a Company Commander of the 109th Transportation Company. Our mission was to deliver bulk petroleum products throughout Southern Germany.

During my 21 months in Germany, the Cuban Missile crises and the Kennedy assassination occurred. We were always on "Alert" and for a cold war period of time it was as hard as I have ever worked. It was here that I realized that I was better in the work-a-day world than in school. I have a very strong work ethic and "can do" attitude and my potential really started to develop in the service. I am forever grateful to the U.S. Army for taking a young kid who had kind of lost his fastball and confidence, and making him into a man.

When I finished my tour of duty on March 10, 1964, I was ready to come back to the States and hit the ground running. Even though there was the adversity of a broken engagement and a job lined up that did not materialize, I knew, after all that I had experienced in Germany, that I was ready for whatever the next step was going to be.

Time for the Real World

Through a series of iterations I found my way into the world of "Industrial Relations," which became "Personnel," which evolved into "Human Resources." The next 40 years seemingly went by as quickly as the next few paragraphs.

It would take volumes to capture the essence of this phenomenal span of experience. Suffice it to say I found the girl of my dreams, married, and had two great sons, started off in the employment agency business, gravitated to the corporate world of HR staffing, mainly with the vibrant Digital Equipment Corporation (the hottest company on earth from the mid-'70s to the early '90s, and I was right in the middle of it), and finally finished my career hooked up with an HR icon, Jack Erdlen.

Erdlen and I owned a human resources consulting firm that was leading edge in every way. We rode a wave for seven years, and then sold it to a public company, and at 56 years-old I was financially secure enough to be able to retire. The 56 year battle, with all that potential, finally was won. I had at last climbed to the top of the mountain. My family would be financially secure for years to come. What a euphoric feeling for a kid who grew up very middle class while surrounded by the opulence that was displayed in Newton.

I hung around for a few more years as a consultant and then faded off into the distance to just do what I wanted to do – on my terms and on my time. The high point was winning the John D. Erdlen Five-Star Award in 2003 from the Northeast Human Resources Association, which validated my work in the field of human resources for the span of 40 years. The low point was the passing away of my partner, friend, and mentor, Jack Erdlen, from colon cancer on November 13, 1999. I will always be indebted to Jack for showing me the way. I miss him a lot.

Some of the highlights and accomplishments of the last 40 years are outlined below to give you a flavor of my involvement throughout the years leading to eventual retirement.

Professional

- ◆ Nine years in the Employment Agency business
- ◆ Eleven years in corporate America with Laboratory for Electronics (one year) and Digital Equipment Corporation (ten years – Finance & Administration Staffing Manager; Corporate College Relations Manager; Manager of Employment Advertising; Customer Service Field Staffing Manager)
- ◆ Twenty years Human Resources Consulting as a Vice President with Costello, Erdlen & Co.; a partner with Bograd, Gatti & Associates; a partner in Bograd, Gatti, Hegan & Associates; a partner in The Erdlen, Bograd Group, which became Strategic Outsourcing, Inc., and which was later acquired by a public company, Romac, Inc. The major success player was Strategic Outsourcing Inc., owned by Barry Bograd and Jack Erdlen. SOI had a consulting practice that included the largest HR contract service in the U.S., outplacement, outsourcing, retained search, compensation and benefits, reference checking, along with creating and managing the largest Human Resources Professional Association in the East – The Northeast Human Resources Association which currently has more than 4,500 members.
- ◆ Consultant for Studley Associates; Gatti & Company
- ◆ President and CEO of King & Bishop, helping to reorganize during the recessional period of time.

All in all, I've had a 40 year career, mainly in staffing and HR consulting, culminating with winning the John D. Erdlen Five-Star Award in 2003. This award, which is the Northeast Human Resources Association's highest honor, is bestowed annually to an individual, organization or association that has demonstrated a humanistic concern for employees and society and a deep respect for the human resources profession. The nomination letter stated "your nomination is in recognition of your leadership within the human resources community, your long history of assisting HR professionals in their career development and in 'giving back' within the profession and within the community. It is also fitting to honor you as a founder of NEHRA." Receiving this award was my finest professional hour.

- ◆ Professional Associations (Board of Directors)
  - Bentley College Human Resources Advisory Board
  - Northeast Human Resources Association
  - Human Resources Council

Personal

- ◆ Married to Elaine for 40 years
- ◆ Son, Jeff, is a Vice President, Managing ERISA Consultant with N.Y. Life Investment Management LLC Retirement Plan Services; his wife, Karen, is the Second VP, Marketing at the same firm. They have three children: Nicholas, age nine, Emma, age five, and Harrison, age one.
- ◆ Son, Mark, is a Guidance Counselor and Soccer Coach at John Stark Regional High School in New Hampshire; his wife, Brooke, is a high school Mathematics teacher and Cheerleader Coach. They have one daughter, Samantha, who is 20 months-old.

I've always "kind of" majored in extra-curricula activities. This goes back to school days and continues on throughout my adult life even to this day in my retirement years. Here are just some of the activities that I've been involved with:

- Newton Jaycees – Voted one of Outstanding Young Men of the Year in 1966
- Newton Association for Responsible Civic Progress, a political action group
- Umpire and referee, Newton City Leagues
- Player, Softball Leagues
- Framingham United Soccer – Coach, Board of Directors, Treasurer
- Framingham Pop Warner – Coach, Board of Directors, Treasurer
- Temple Beth Am Basketball League – Coach, Board of Directors – TV Sportscaster
- Public Broadcasting Channel 2 – Auction On-Air Volunteer
- Middlesex News – Sports Columnist
- Community Cablevision – TV Producer and on-air talent: Dateline Framingham; Sporting Events; Elections Live
- Campaign Manager – State Representative and Selectman's race
- Salute to Framingham Dinner – Master of Ceremonies
- Salute to Framingham Award Winner – 1998
- Town of Framingham Personnel Board; Parks & Recreation Commissioner; Finance Committee
- Newton High School Class of 1957 Reunion Committee, Chairperson

- ◆ Owner (with Jack Erdlen) of several race horses
- ◆ Owner North-South Soccer Camp
- ◆ Owner Lights, Camera, Action – TV production company

These activities, coupled with a full professional career, along with being very involved with my two boys as they grew up – gave me cause for concern as I approached retirement. Since I get bored easily, how was I going to fill the time? As I stated earlier, my biggest fear was sitting on my big leather chair staring at the four walls. I was determined I would not let that happen to me.

Retirement, or a reasonable facsimile thereof, began the moment Jack Erdlen and I sold our company in March, 1996. Working for the new owner for the next three and one-half years was not what I'd call fun. It was not their fault. I was just too much of a control freak, and they were making all the decisions. In my mind most of the decisions were counter to how I would have handled things. After Jack Erdlen died in November of 1999, it just made sense to begin the process of ending the relationship with the new owners. To their credit, they never missed a payment and were honorable to the end. The relationship ended in June of 2000.

Okay, I know it's taken me forever to get into the meat of this chapter – retirement. But, I wanted you, the reader, to get a sense of what went on during the career part of my life. I'm really not a hobbyist, so as my career wound down, my fear was that, like a diver who comes up too quickly in the water and gets the bends, I would shut off my involvements and have literally nothing to do.

Retirement

I'm not sure when retirement began. I'm not sure if it even has. The past three and one-half years since retirement have been almost as busy as before retirement. My three areas of concentration have been:

♦ Coaching Varsity Football at Newton South High School
I've done this for seven years, six days-a-week from the end
of August through Thanksgiving. I always wanted to coach
football at this level, and as an insulin-dependent diabetic (my
biggest albatross), it also provided good exercise as well as
the pleasure of working for a friend whom I've known for 53
years as head coach. I also spent three afternoons a week
from January to June monitoring a weight-lifting program. So
you can see, coaching has been like a full-time job.

♦ Human Resources
I spent the year 2000 consulting for Studley & Associates;
2001 for Gatti & Company; and 2002 as President & CEO
for King & Bishop. The years 2003 & 2004 were the first
since 1964 that I wasn't formally involved in the field of HR,
although I still get calls to be "of counsel" on a *pro bono* basis
to several companies and people in the HR arena. I find it
challenging and flattering that people still seek my advice. It's
good for the ego – which can get deflated very quickly when
you segue into the retirement years. Sound familiar?

♦ Finance Committee – Town of Framingham
In September 2003, I was appointed to the prestigious Finance
Committee. This, too, is like a full-time job, and is very time
consuming. It's the financial watchdog for the town, requiring
making presentations at Town Meetings. I also hosted an
election night television program.

And, finally, collaborating with Martha R. A. Fields on this book
about retirement. It's been a lifelong ambition of mine to write a book.
Hence, with the guidance of this eminent author, we have been
immersed in the creation of the pages in front of you. It's a tremendous

challenge, but one that I relish. I do hope these examples of what you can do in your retirement years makes a difference for you, the reader.

Oh, I almost forgot. I was the assistant coach (my son, Jeff, was the Head Coach) for a second-grade spring soccer team in the Hopkinton (Massachusetts) Youth Soccer League this past spring. My grandson was on the team. It's starting all over again. He also is playing Pop Warner Football and we run every Sunday to watch his team play.

So when I stop and think about it, retirement is just a word. I'm not making much money at this stage of my life, but my days are full. My parents just turned 92 and 91, and celebrated their 70th wedding anniversary in October 2004. As an only child, I take them to doctors, shopping, and the like. That too is a major commitment, but I'm blessed to have them at this stage of my life.

It's been a long and tough ride through the years, with a great many roller coaster situations. But I got through the tube and now I'm on the back nine, heading home. I look at my life as one of excitement, involvement, and true blessings. What happens from here? Who knows? I'm always willing to take a risk and try new things. I love my leather chair – but I'm not quite ready to make it my permanent home…not just yet.

In a nutshell

Barry keeps turning over the rocks to see what's underneath. He knows his limits, but his passion for life makes him exceed them every time. Just when you think he's ready to say goodbye and slow down, he is back at it again.

- He always had a fear of retiring cold turkey and sitting on the leather chair looking at the four walls. This fear motivated him to make sure that didn't happen.

- He was always involved in a multitude of activities since his childhood, and this involvement carried over into retirement.

- He was always a curious sort of person, and was not afraid to ask why or venture into new vistas.

- He is involved with many activities, including taking care of elderly parents and becoming involved with grandchildren's events.

- He bought a second home on a lake that required new involvement and activities.

- After retirement, he took his hobby of football and became a varsity high school football coach for seven years.

- After his company was sold, he worked for the acquiring firm for three and one-half years, and subsequently consulted in the same industry for three more years. He eased out of his life-long profession into retirement.

- As an insulin-dependent diabetic, and prone to high blood pressure, he became vigilant about his health.

- He always had a passion for writing. He wrote several published articles and newspaper columns over the years, but always wanted to write a book. This challenging project kept him actively engaged for a couple of years.

- After retirement, he was appointed to the Finance Committee in Framingham, Massachusetts. This prestigious town committee meets so often, it's almost like a full-time job.

☛ Barry has kept busy in retirement by involving himself with interesting projects and people. He has found meaningful places to go and things to do.

☛ He suggests not making too large a commitment, and leaving yourself some wiggle room so if you decide to drop an activity, it will be okay on either end.

☛ He recommends maintaining friendships. Go to lunch or dinner with old colleagues, even if just for reminiscing. Hook up with high school, college and business friends and associates. Get involved with reunions, just for the camaraderie.

2

That Crazy
Lady from
Framingham

When I asked former State Representative, Barbara E. Gray, how she liked retirement, she bellowed, "*I hate it!*" And so began my wild and woolly interview with this feisty 77 year-old diminutive lady who took Metrowest by storm. So I warn you, buckle up and hold on, because the irreverent Ms. Gray is about to pontificate.

As a matter of fact, asking you to buckle your seatbelt is quite apropos, for Barbara was the key reason the Massachusetts seat belt law was passed. Called "that crazy lady from Metrowest" by radio personality, Howie Carr, and "the strange lady from Framingham" (among other things), by the venerable late radio pitchman, Jerry Williams, Barbara Gray forged a 24 year state house career that was unparalleled in the fight for women's rights, especially in the areas of Safety and Health issues.

She was a one woman wrecking crew when she wanted to get her point across. She always seemed to be on a mission, and wouldn't stop until she got what she wanted. But we get ahead of ourselves.

Born in New York City, the only child of a fervent Republican and successful stock broker father and closet-Democrat mother, Barbara was truly a mixture of both parents. As a matter of fact, she began her political career as a Republican and ended it as a Democrat. You can almost see what you are in for as you read further. She was called "brash" – maybe because she was always competing with her parents, or it could be because of her upbringing in New York City.

As a youngster, she always seemed to be running hard to catch up or to position herself to get her parents' attention. Barbara learned to be quite independent, for her folks traveled a great deal, leaving her with relatives. They also had full-time help to take care of her.

She discussed world affairs with her father a great deal. Barbara explained, "I wanted to show him how smart I was. It was my father who honed my debating skills and mind. My father was one of those chaps who rose from errand boy on Wall Street to partner at Wood, Struthers and Winthrop brokerage firm. Dad was very successful and well respected in his field.

"I was fortunate to be born into very successful stock. My grandfather was a lawyer and an engineer from Kansas who designed the Merritt Parkway in New York. My mother was a star athlete and debater, who never worked outside the home. Tennis was the common recreational activity of my parents. They also played championship duplicate bridge together. My mother was very social and loved parties. She loved to mix and laugh with people."

I think that's where Barbara got her love of parties and people. Given her background, roots, and determination she was destined to be someone special. "If you are always on the same side with people you interface with," said Barbara, "then you are not growing, thinking, or reaching out to be receptive to new ideas."

When I asked her if she knew when she went to college she would end up with a political career, her answer was, "absolutely not!" She went to the prestigious Connecticut College for Women (which has since become co-ed) for several reasons. First and foremost was "to pass." However, a close second reason was "to go to as many parties at men's colleges as I could, and third was to get married and have children," Barbara said.

"The one thing I became passionate about at college was singing. I sang in an augmented octet and loved it. You might say that was the key to my political future, because politicians love to sing. We all love to perform. We are all actors or actresses of some kind, as evidenced by the annual St. Patrick's Day Roast at the Ironworkers Hall in South Boston hosted by Senator Jack Hart.

"I was not very political at Connecticut College," said Barbara, "although I did go to a few political rallies. I also was not a strong advocate for women's issues as a college student.

"Having majored in Social Anthropology and International Relations, I felt compelled to go to Oxford in England the summer after graduation to get a degree, which, although it looked great on my CV, didn't mean a thing. Immediately after, I worked for the American Association for the United Nations. I was going to save the world. Not long after that I found a job in the advertising department of *Coronet* and *Esquire* magazines."

It was all good training, but a relationship with Dick Gray, who had landed a job with the Yale Lock Co. in Connecticut took Barbara to Hartford, where she was hired as Society Editor at the *Hartford Times* newspaper. "I wrote columns about events that I never went to, and about people who I didn't know, and everyone loved it," said Barbara. "I faked it," and laughingly stated, "I've faked it ever since!

"When you work for the media, you realize a few things: number one is that the media is lazy; secondly, they take what you give them; and finally, if you return their phone calls right away, they think you're wonderful. All they want is for you to be brief and succinct so that they can get off the phone. They really don't care about you, they are just looking for a good story, which is really their role. I've kept my newspaper experience in mind throughout my political years."

I asked Barbara how she ended up in Framingham. "Very simple," she said, "I got married, which if you remember was one of my major goals. Dick was a sales rep and got a job in Massachusetts and we moved to this area. We moved to Newton first, and 55 years ago came to Framingham. I really didn't need to work. We had two kids when we came here, and eventually had two more. I didn't work outside the home, but along with some friends, I formed the League of Women (Vultures, she laughingly calls it) Voters. It seemed that people in office could do just about anything they pleased. There was not much accountability, so we created a group to act as a watchdog, developed a 'do you know your town?' study, and tried to help people know about government while encouraging them to participate.

"Once I got into politics, I decided to take it to the next step. I became aware of a particular developer who was building hundreds of houses in Framingham, and I believed he was raping the land. It was time for me to spring into action. I filed to run for the Redevelopment Authority. Before the election, I became aware that there was going to be an opening on the Planning Board, which had even more impact. And so I crossed out Redevelopment Authority and threw my hat in the ring for the Planning Board. I won the seat and held it for 11 years. I was hooked, and there was no turning back."

"But how did you get to the legislature?" I asked Barbara. "Well," she said, "my first husband, Dick Gray, said I was spending a lot of time on volunteer activities, and why didn't I want to do something I would get paid for? I said, Okay, I'll run for the state legislature, which at that time paid a whopping $11,000 a year. Being my father's daughter, I ran as a Republican against a sitting Democrat in a double district. I caught them with their political signs down. I was a liberal Republican, and with the help of the Kennedy campaign people, we ousted the incumbent Democrat, a well-known local attorney.

"As a Republican legislator I had no place to go. I was never going to be a Chair – certainly not in Massachusetts. I was never going to be in leadership. I had a blast! I filed hundreds of bills every year (24 years to be exact). I was the only woman on the House Committee of Ways and Means for ten years. The leadership used to cringe when they saw me coming. My mantra was Health and Safety. I was a zealot. I'm proud to say I was responsible for such laws as seat belts, margarine in restaurants, jet ski protection, motorcycle helmets, domestic violence prevention, no fault divorce, health services for women in prison, to name just a few. They were all new ideas. There was no one else in the Massachusetts legislature who espoused these ideas. I was a great plagiarizer. I would take ideas from out of state or from abroad – I traveled a lot.

"I had the most fun when I incurred the wrath of talk radio hosts Jerry Williams and Howie Carr," said Barbara. This little lady from Framingham was taking on the top dogs in radio, and was not going to back down. "The more they came after me, the better I liked it," said Barbara. 'Barbara Gray' became a household name. Monikers such as, "Holy Pest," "Battling Barbara," "Eminence Grise," and "St. Barbara of Gray," wafted across the airways.

"My image became bigger than life," said Barbara. "I got a kick out of this. It only strengthened my resolve to dig my heels in on my issues. By the way, all my causes were eventually passed and became law.

"I have always been a risk taker and a rebel," said Barbara. "The biggest political scare came in 1990, when I lost in the Republican primary to Tom Tierney. It was the only time that I've ever been beaten. I was devastated. How did that happen?

"Undaunted, I came right back as a write-in candidate on the Democratic side. Well, my mother was a Democrat, and I was truly a liberal Republican. There were no other Democratic candidates. Fortunately I beat my Republican challenger, Mr. Tierney, who had beaten me in the primary. That was my last loss. Losing is not very good for the psyche. If you lose anything in life, a job, a loved one, an election, take it upon yourself to seek counseling. It will definitely help you get through it.

"While I was spending my 24 years in the legislature, I made time to be involved in many activities in my home town, in things I cared passionately about. I served as a trustee at the Danforth Museum of Art and the New England Wildflower Society. I created many human service organizations, including the Wayside Youth & Family Network Advocates, Inc., Women's Independence Network, and the Samaritans. I also stayed in close contact with anything musical, which, as you remember, I adored."

I asked Barbara how she knew it was time for retirement. "Very simple," she said, "I backed the wrong horse for speaker. I supported Richie Voke over Tom Finneran. Tom lined up all the Republicans and key Democrats with promises of committee Chairmanships. I was Chair of the Natural Resources and Agriculture Committee (a very prestigious position), and I knew, with Finneran in, I would lose that post. I had sponsored legislation to include the Open Space Bond Bill, the River Protection Act, along with Title V – all kinds of environmental things. I honestly felt that I couldn't serve under the type of autocratic leadership that I knew Tommy Finneran would exercise. I love Tommy as a person. We women legislators voted that he had the cutest 'tush' in the House, but it just wasn't going to work for me. In retrospect, every sitting Democrat who backed Richie Voke lost their Chairs, or have no office, or are sitting in the hall.

"The handwriting was on the wall. I loved the institution too much to participate under that type of regime. I truly believed that the previous speakers were not vindictive. They would allow much more debate on the floor. Hence, in 1996, I made a conscious decision to leave the legislature. I might have stayed four to six more years if things had broken differently.

"In the eight years since I left the House," continued Barbara, "many people have asked me how I like retirement. I answer in the same way that I answered to you, "*I hate it.*" I was very invested in the legislature, and had a tremendous feeling of accomplishment. But I had a feeling there was still a lot more to do. With a lot of penned up energy I became trustee of this and that, and became active on the volunteer boards of the organizations that I started. I have always loved traveling, so I did that with my second husband, Norm Gardner.

"It's not easy trying to find the core value of one's life when you have been the central part of something. I really don't think that I've found it yet; I'm still searching. There is always a new seed to cultivate. While you are involved with your occupation, it's important to stay active with other activities, because eventually they may flip-flop and become the major things of your life. I'm still campaigning for people and causes I believe in. I was elected as a Town Meeting member and have stayed active in town affairs. It's almost like coming full circle.

"Always seek new vistas," advises Barbara. "After 55 years I'm leaving my beloved Framingham. It's in good hands. I'm moving to my summer home 'down the Cape' in Wellfleet, Massachusetts. I haven't found my niche there yet, but I'm sure I'll make trouble there too. They have a lot of issues that Framingham once had. I want new challenges and new friends. (I'll keep the old ones too.) I'm also going to spend winters in Menlo Park, California near my family. This, too, is very exciting for me.

"Financially I'm okay," said Barbara. "Being on a pension (the legislative salary eventually went to $57,000 in my last years) is certainly not like being on a salary. But I am probably healthier than ever before. My husband and I are both heart patients, but we take good care of ourselves. I truly think it's time to spend more time with my family at this time of my life. I only wish they were closer." (Sadly her husband, Norm Gardner, died of cardiac arrest four days after this interview.)

Finally, I asked Barbara what advice would she give people reading this book on retirement. "Never say the word 'retirement,'" she replied. "'Retire,' as defined by the dictionary talks about retreating or pulling back. But I think of these years as a time for expansion. It's like any other career move. Think about it at least five years ahead of time. Decide, number one, that you really want to do it, and number two, that you'll do it at your own pace, speed and timing. It still will hit you, but prepare yourself, your partner, your spouse, and your family. There will be changes. You will need some help. Continue to have fun in your life. Pace yourself, and don't try to do everything at once and enjoy."

Barbara reflects, "I guess that I really wouldn't have changed anything in my life. I wish Richie Voke had won that Speakership, for I would have remained in the House a little longer. My legacy is to take young minds and relate to them, and reach out continuously. I may go back to teaching or lecturing. I'll always be feisty and rebellious – tell me to do something and I'll probably do the opposite. That's just who I am. It's gotten me into a little trouble in my life…but not enough. I'm still going to keep at it."

Go Barbara, Go!

 ## In a nutshell

Barbara thrives on controversy. She sometimes likes to place the proverbial bomb in a strategic place and sit back and watch everybody react to it. She is an intellectual prankster.

- In her early days, she was feisty and often rebellious. She continued this pattern with a wink and a twinkle in her eye into the next phase of her life.

- She became active in her new residence of Wellfleet when she moved to Cape Cod at age 77.

- As she ended her Massachusetts State House career, she expanded her volunteer activities.

- In order to be near her children and grandchildren, she travels to Menlo Park, California and spends every winter with them.

- Barbara just can't help becoming involved. She has an insatiable curiosity. She also is very opinionated.

- She has always been very social, and her social activities have kept her quite busy and active in her later years.

- She is a "contra," sometimes for contra's sake. I like to call her a rebel with a cause!

3

The Transition
Was Seamless

The neat two-family house tucked into a well-manicured section down the street and in the shadows of Harvard Square in Cambridge, Massachusetts, was really not a surprise to me. However, when I came up the stairs to the second level to conduct my interview, I was astounded by the rehab work that Gloria Thompson had done on her home. But as I ascended the black spiral staircase, I came upon the *piece de resistance*, a third floor oasis that just blew me away.

The third floor, which originally had been a crawl space, had been converted into an amazing office/apartment. That's how Gloria began her second career, oh so many years ago, by rehabbing her own house. But, we are way ahead of ourselves. We'll come back to this part of our story a little later in the chapter.

This delightful, reserved woman was the daughter of West Indian parents, who believed that education of all of their children was the key to success. Brought up in the Roxbury section of Boston, Gloria is quite proud of her heritage and quickly pointed out to me when I asked if she was brought up in Boston that, no, her roots were in Roxbury.

Ms. Thompson graduated from a three-year program at the Melrose-Wakefield Hospital Nursing School with an R.N. Certificate. Unfortunately, she ran out of money after the second year, so she joined the military at school to help pay the expenses of her third year. This R.O.T.C. program allowed her to become a Second Lieutenant upon graduation. It not only helped pay for the last year of her education, but gave her a great start on her chosen career – nursing.

She went to Fort Sam Houston in Texas for medical basic training, with the thought of potentially ending up in Vietnam. This was during 1966-67, and the action was hot and heavy in the Far East. She was prepared to go overseas, but was assigned to the Walter Reed Army Hospital in Washington, D.C. instead. It was there that she married her high school sweetheart, Alvin.

Gloria truly enjoyed the military experience. It taught her discipline, which has translated to regimenting her life by responsible, orderly living. This was a carryover from her childhood where her parents were quite strict, and very religious, as well as charitable Christians. As a 21 year-old officer, Gloria learned to delegate responsibility. She quickly realized that one does not have to do everything yourself – that you could delegate and expect the work would be done. You could hold people accountable.

"Here I was, a 21 year-old woman, with Sergeants and Sergeant-Majors twice my age reporting to me," said Gloria, "and I was responsible for their actions. I always treated them with dignity. I never ruled with an iron hand, but I got things done. I was insistent, persistent, but gentle and kind."

Working at Walter Reed during this historical time was quite emotional. She worked on a floor with returning wounded Vietnam soldiers. Some had lost extremities, and some were on the verge of dying. She cradled the wounded at night and gave them medication to ease their pain. They sometimes cried out, "Ma" as they died in her arms. This made an ever-lasting impression on her. It didn't matter what color they were, or where they came from, or if they were rich or poor. They were human beings, and that's all that mattered. She teared up as she recalled this part of her life, almost 40 years ago.

Her two years in the service ended, and back to Roxbury she went with loads of hands-on experience. Her husband, Alvin, who later became a prominent State Representative from Cambridge, worked two jobs and Gloria worked part-time at Massachusetts General Hospital. In 1971, they pooled their money and bought the house Gloria still lives in from the heirs of a deceased uncle. Gloria worked at the Mass General for seven years as a medical-surgical nurse. Subsequently, she went back to school at the University of Massachusetts at the Boston campus, and received her Bachelor's degree in Psychology. This allowed her to become a core evaluation nurse in the Cambridge School Department. She spent 28 years in this system.

Gloria loved children, and working with them all those years was a joy and a blessing. But she found her fellow employees somewhat pretentious. Many had Ph.D.s and double Master's Degrees and wore it on their sleeves. Gloria's co-workers in the school department unfortunately were condescending, so she really didn't make many close friends. "We were cordial, but I did not form great friendships," said Gloria. "It was truly a working relationship. There were very few minorities in positions of power."

Their erudite attitudes can be attributed to the fact that Gloria was a person of color, and that they had fancy educations. "However, the fact that my husband was a well-known State Legislator allowed me to be haughty right back," said Gloria. It was not a comfortable situation, to say the least. Interpreting medical data was her expertise and no one else in the system could do that. Eventually Gloria went to Cambridge College and received a Master's Degree in Education.

Gloria's parents were uneducated and she reiterated that education was a primary value in their lives. She carried this value over to her own three children, including caring for a nephew who came to live with them when he was 14 years-old.

A benefit of working for the school department was that she was home by 2:30 p.m. when her kids came home. She made sure there was no nonsense. There was to be order in the home. Dinner was at 6:00 p.m. and then homework, followed by a little downtime, and then to bed. Those were the rules!

Due to her husband Alvin's prominence, Gloria had the privilege of being a guest at the White House, of attending two Presidential Inaugurations, and dining with eminent personalities, including Nelson Mandela, Desmond Tutu, and former Democratic National Chairman, Ron Brown.

Alvin unfortunately passed on four years ago from a heart attack. Gloria misses him terribly. During Alvin's ten years in the House, the day-to-day grind of campaigning took up a great deal of time in their lives. However, Gloria still made time to volunteer in the following organizations and groups:

- ◆ Cambridge Board of Trustees
- ◆ Cambridge Camping Association
- ◆ Shady Hill Board of Overseers
- ◆ Church Choir
- ◆ Church Board of Directors
- ◆ Sunday School Teacher

In the 1980s, when real estate was hot, getting your real estate license was in vogue. So, one summer, while her kids were in camp, Gloria obtained her license, never thinking she would do much with it, for she was too busy with her school job. To this day she has never sold a piece of property as an agent for someone else, but she made a lot of referrals. She was known in Cambridge for her involvement in the church and because of Alvin's political life. Since she was also known as a reliable person, people sought her out for advice. "Should I sell my property? What should I do?" they would ask.

A key component of Gloria's transition into the second phase of her life was the formulation of a "ladies" investment group many years ago. This consisted of 15 women, ages 35 to 88, from all walks of life. Over the years they had over 30 guest speakers. The discussions centered on such topics as mutual funds, long-term care insurance, irrevocable and revocable trusts, and virtually anything that would safeguard their money.

Everyone in the group now has a will or a trust. They have all bought houses, and have made future plans. Some have multiple homes. One woman opened up her own business. They have a social outing twice a year. Gloria said that was another reason she segued into the real estate business. "When my lady friends and their friends decided to either buy or sell property, they came to me," she said. "I reiterate, I have never actually sold a home, but I have referred people and developed properties."

I asked her if, since she retired in 2002, after 28 years in the school system, was she in a career change or a retirement mode? She answered, "a little bit of both. I manage my own substantial holdings, but could take a trip for a month without the roof falling in. Everything is geared to run on its own with the assistance of my sister, who does the same thing.

"I got the bug to rehab houses when I first did my own, oh so many years ago. I have bought properties that I have totally gutted and rehabbed. I create an office in the property, don a hard hat, and direct the operation. I keep the workers rotating – there is no time wasted! It's not much different than when I was a Lieutenant almost 40 years ago. The same disciplined principles apply. I stay until the last nail is pounded.

"My responsibility to the tenants is being a landlord, a maintenance company, a gardener – whatever it takes. I inherited some properties and bought some on my own. It's a little like monopoly. Once you get into it, if you stay on course, it's just a lot of follow-up and follow-through. You must maintain good relationships with your resources. We do a lot of business with banks. They have been very cooperative. Three lending institutions that have been very helpful are the East Cambridge Savings Bank, Cambridge Savings Bank, and the Heritage Mortgage Company in Newton. Once you have one property it's easy to get others."

I asked her whether or not she misses the school system. She replied, "I miss the children, but not the people I worked with." Gloria considers herself semi-retired. She loves to travel, with cruises being her specialty. She employs a bookkeeper, a CPA, an accountant, an assistant, a housekeeper and gardeners. The lawns of all her properties are immaculate and extremely well manicured. This is a signature of hers.

Some of her final thoughts were that she would like to buy more properties in the future. She remains practical, curious and very disciplined. She won't let issues of color or discrimination stop her; she will continue to treat people like people – with dignity. She advises people to use what they have to their best advantage. What really bothers her is that she has lost some friends as she has become more affluent.

Gloria Thompson is very comfortable with who she is. She truly believes in the power of prayer.

While I was in her office, the phone never stopped ringing. She is quite adept at multi-tasking, and handled each call professionally and with an air of confidence, but she never gave me the impression that she wasn't focused on our discussion. I came away from my afternoon interview impressed with this woman who has made a seamless transition from one career to another and still has had time to "retire."

Gloria Thompson is a role model for all.

 In a nutshell

Gloria's style is one of understatement. She made the transition to her next phase seem transparent. This lady though is the strong, silent type who has the ability to multi-task with ease, and who is always in control.

- Gloria is a detailed and meticulous person. These characteristics developed with her upbringing, were evidenced in the manner in which she brought up her children, and finally transferred to the way she manages her business.
- She balances her leisure travel with the rigors of her business.
- Gloria has always been focused and disciplined. She is a good learner. She has a tremendous desire to attempt new things. She is a strong, but quiet leader.

- As witnessed by all she has accomplished in life, she has never been afraid to take a risk. She has the power of her convictions.

- She turned her talent of re-habbing properties into a profitable and rewarding next phase of her life.

- Gloria learned to lead and delegate at an early age. She was always mature beyond her years. People seemed to gravitate to her for advice.

- She is insistent and persistent, but gentle and kind. She is well networked; everyone in the community knows Gloria.

4

The Quintessential Retirement Couple

This delightful couple planned their retirement in 1993, and almost 10 years to the day, held hands crossing the finish line to begin the next phase of their lives. We are addressing their story as a couple because of the uniqueness of their journey.

Their lives began in two very different worlds, and eventually evolved to the intertwined existence it is today. They have only been retired 15 months, and although they would deny it, they have accomplished more in that time than most people could given several more years.

In the 16th year of a second marriage, their love and respect for each other was quite evident as I interviewed them. He at age 65 and she at age 55 have created a new life in retirement that will challenge their interesting lives during their work life. Let us go back in time to see how this union evolved. We will begin with Ellie.

Ellie Beth graduated from Mount Holyoke College, a renowned center for learning, with a degree in Political Science. Government and politics have permeated her life in one form or another throughout the years. She was all set to work for the Lieutenant Governor Frank Sargent's re-election committee (a paid gig) when she graduated, but two weeks before she was to start, she was told that the job had been given to the wife of a wealthy contributor, who had volunteered to do it for nothing. They said that if she would do it for free, she could have the job. It was not an auspicious beginning to a public service career that would span the next 33 years.

Ellie found her first job with a television/radio rep firm, and then followed that with the position of Assistant to the Director of a state-run mental health center in Boston. She spent a great deal of time writing grant applications, supervising staff, and defending the budget on Beacon Hill. This was her first foray into the public sector, but certainly it would not be her last.

Eventually motherhood would call, and she stopped working to have two children and be a Scituate stay-at-home mom to Michael and Laura. While beginning her family, Ellie joined the League of Women Voters, where she could keep her mind active and meet interesting people. She got a part-time job writing for the local newspaper, covering School Committee, Selectmen, and Town Meetings. She become well known in the community through her reporting. She could see the issues, condense them, and understand what needed to be accomplished. All of this whet her appetite for the eventual next step.

Ellie was recruited to run for selectman opposing a two-term incumbent. Talented people were running her campaign, and amazingly she toppled the favorite to win the seat. Her cause or mantra was "for the good of the town." There was a great deal of contentiousness on the board, and through a quirk of fate, three months after her election, this rookie selectman became Chair of the Board. Within a few years, this enterprising young woman had risen to President of the County State Selectmen's Associations. There was no stopping her now.

When Ellie's daughter, Laura, was three years-old, she would walk around with a pocketbook on her shoulder. People would ask her if she was going shopping like her mommy. "Oh no," she said. "I'm going to a meeting!" Ellie in essence was a stay-at-home mom who rarely stayed at home. She was involved up to the hilt. She was heavily invested in the statewide organization MMA (Massachusetts Municipal Association).

With all the contacts she was making, she was the object of many recruiting advances. She finally succumbed and joined the Massachusetts Department of Revenue as a consultant in their local services division, where she specialized in management studies for cities and towns. She did this for a couple of years on a 20 hour-a-week basis, when she was recruited again as a consultant in the private sector to write charters, handle financial and management challenges, and be involved in personnel issues.

Ellie was a generalist who hired experts to supplement and augment their consulting practice. One of the experts the firm hired was Harvey Beth, who was a top consultant in the field of public finance. At the same time, Ellie was going through a divorce. Shortly after the break-up, she started dating Harvey, who had also been divorced, and in 1989, they wed.

Harvey moved to Scituate to be with his new family. Ellie had two children, at that time ages 14 and 11. Harvey's two children, Geoffrey and Deborah, were ten years older and had already left the nest. Harvey became a stabilizing force, especially with Ellie's young daughter. All seemed to be headed in the right direction for the newly married couple.

However, one month after the marriage, Ellie was diagnosed with breast cancer, and a day later Harvey's father passed away. Business at the consulting firm, where she had become a partner, dropped off and things certainly were looking glum. Part of Ellie's consulting role had been to create a capital improvements plan for the Town of Plymouth, and when she saw an ad for an Assistant Executive Secretary in that town, she jumped at it. Ninety-eight people applied for the job, and in 1990, she was hired. That began a 14 year love affair with America's first town.

Her first assignment was to help write a new charter, which created a Town Manager form of government. She subsequently was named Assistant Town Manager, and a few years later, in 1998, through a series of events, was promoted to Town Manager, with the retirement plan still in play. So Ellie knew that five years down the road, retirement loomed on the horizon.

Ellie's philosophy on reaching the top is interesting. "Women never think that they are ready for their job, while men think they are born ready," she said. "Women have done it to themselves. They have the 'Wizard of Oz Syndrome' — do not pull back the curtain because you will see the real me. Men are raised to believe that they can do anything. Women are raised to believe that they have to prove themselves" she says.

Harvey tends to disagree with Ellie's theory that only women have the 'Wizard of Oz Syndrome.' He believes that it is shared equally among men and women. "We all have our own insecurities," he said That takes Ellie through a successful career ladder. We will revisit her after we chronicle Harvey's work life.

Harvey Beth, the less outgoing, Omar Sharif-looking partner, is none-the-less passionate in his views. An only child, he began his career as a 12 year-old selling newspapers in the heart of Boston on Albany Street behind Boston City Hospital, where his father worked. Harvey came from a poor background, which meant he had to make his own way in life. There would be no gimmes for this young lad.

After a couple of years at Boston Latin High School, he transferred to Roxbury Memorial, and later attended Northeastern University's Co-op program. At that time, college tuition was $752 a year, and in the Co-op program, students attended school for ten weeks and then worked for ten weeks. The working weeks helped to pay the freight, as well as provide a great education and diversity. Harvey majored in Accounting and minored in Economics, and also enjoyed the Arts.

After graduating in 1960, he was hired by Peat, Marwick, a very prestigious public accounting firm. He liked the fact that he could wear blue-striped shirts, and not have to be robotic and wear the "white shirt" uniform. This company did things a little more out of the box – more to Harvey's liking. After his first six months, he received a battlefield promotion and became a Senior, and eventually a Supervisor in charge of engagements.

He grew a great deal in his seven years with Peat. He took Morse Shoe public, received his MBA from Babson College, became a member of the Finance Committee in his new hometown of Natick, Massachusetts, and concentrated his practice on electronics, shoes, and retail. He was on his way.

Peat rewarded him with two promotional offers: one was managing the Anchorage, Alaska office. But when he saw that the price of lettuce in Alaska in 1967 was $2.67 a head, he politely declined the offer. The other offer was a partnership in New York City, but that was not for this Boston boy. If you know large firms, once you start turning down promotions, it's time to pack up and leave.

He had several job opportunities, and eventually became CFO of a military electronics firm in Natick, named Sage Labs. They were in the radar business, but also developed one of the first microwave ovens.

At this time of his life Harvey was forming his own political views and values. He was a pacifist who was not interested in war. Most of his friends' concerns centered on pacifism, civil rights, and civil liberties. Sage was centered on the defense industry, and Harvey had an internal conflict with their core values. He believed in electronics for peace. They tried a few ventures, but Sage really made their money in the military electronics business. So he left.

The next eight years were spent as CFO of a wildly popular chain of stores called Paperback Booksmith. This franchise business grew up and down the east coast, while also developing a large distribution entity to supply their franchisees with product. They grew so rapidly that they did it without adequate financing, forcing them to make financial deals to stay in business, and this went against Harvey's grain and ethics. He learned a great deal about business from this experience, but it was time to move to the next phase in his life.

Harvey combined his Finance Committee background with his recent business experience, MBA and CPA, and became the CFO for the Town of Needham, Massachusetts. His role was to clean up the mess that he inherited. The year was 1978. At the time he was also involved in a variety of outside activities that included:

- ♦ Counselor – as a conscientious objector, he counseled people who left the country during the Vietnam War era

- ♦ Drug counselor

- ♦ Founder of an alternative school in Natick, "Vision in Action"

- ♦ Counselor to prisoners returning to the mainstream
- ♦ Volunteer at Discovery House in Framingham, counseling potentially suicidal youngsters. Sometimes he slept overnight at this center.

Harvey's strong and passionate values permeated his life. He really was a social worker at heart and a financial executive by profession.

When I asked Ellie about her outside activities during these years, she stated that her job was that of being a mom, while her outside world included being selectman, participating in kid's activities, and writing for the local newspaper. She also found time to sing in the church choir and with a chorale society. Music has always had a place in her life.

Needham was a culture shock for Harvey. Coming from the world of big business (Paperback Booksmith) to the public sector in the bedroom community of Needham was like hitting a brick wall. He became involved in a great many professional associations, both for the networking exposure and for the opportunity to learn more about the public way of doing things. He quickly straightened out Needham, made a name for himself statewide, and before he knew it, was recruited to become the Director of the Bureau of Accounts in the state's Department of Revenue.

They needed a CPA-type person who knew governmental accounting. Harvey came in as a change agent charged with bringing in electronic and computerized systems, and doing away with the archaic methods that were a symbol of the department for so long. He taught cities' and towns' Treasurer-Collectors new and innovative methods for doing their jobs. He made them accountable, and designed a quarterly reporting system identifying where their money was invested and how much each city and town was earning. This accountability kick made him popular in some quarters, but deemed him a pain in the butt in others.

After seven years, he was tapped by then Governor Dukakis to become CFO at the Department of Transportation. This, claims Harvey, was the worst career move of his life. He could not reconcile his beliefs with the political nature of how they did business. The Director said, "This is the way it is, and you either take it or leave it." Harvey's ethics, as we have seen in the past, forced him to make a move.

He landed in the City of Boston as the Deputy City Auditor, hired by the Mayor Raymond Flynn administration. He spent four years in Boston, with another year and one-half as the Director of Finance for the City of Marlborough.

All of this previous experience prepared him for his final journey through the work world – spending 14 years, from age 51-64 as the Director of Finance (CFO) for the Town of Brookline. "It was the best job I ever had!" said Harvey. He retired in the spring of 2003, after over 40 years in both public and private sectors of business and finance. It was time to move to the next phase of his life.

During his years in Brookline, Harvey's roundtrip commute from Scituate was often three hours. "You just can't get there from here!" he said. The couple always loved the water, so they fell in love with and moved to a condominium at Marina Bay in Quincy. This was their first separation from their "over involvement" in Scituate. Their plans were to make a dramatic change and move to Martha's Vineyard in retirement. They suggest making an interim move first to prepare for the shock of the retirement move.

Remember that Ellie and Harvey were married in 1989, with Harvey moving into Ellie's home in Scituate with her two children – at the time a boy, age 14 and a girl, age 11. In 1992, when they decided that ten years from then they would retire, they had the foresight and wherewithal to build a small vacation house on Martha's Vineyard. "It would be our house, we'd retire there, and we did everything together," they said.

The first day, way back in the '80s, when Harvey dropped in to visit Ellie and her kids, Ellie's daughter was so taken by him that when he left she said, "Mommy, you should marry that man." So she did! When Harvey's daughter was married, Ellie and Harvey's ex-wife were bridesmaids together – both in their frilly pink dresses. When Ellie's daughter got married, Harvey's grandchildren were flower girls. Therefore, as you can see, the family assimilated well throughout the years.

Harvey retired two weeks before Ellie – he in April, she in May of 2003 – right on schedule. They segued to the next phase of their life. Ellie, who is a two-time breast cancer survivor, was well aware that they had a whole lot to do, and she honestly did not know how much time she had to do it in. Harvey, in good health at age 64, wanted to become more involved with a hobby that had been his passion for most of his life. They were revved up for a combination of travel, hobbies, and of course, volunteerism.

Let's see what transpired over their first 15 months of retirement. Take a deep breath and strap on your seatbelt. Here goes....

Harvey had always had a love affair with photography. Being an introvert, and frankly feeling more comfortable in one-on-one situations, photography provided an outlet where he could derive a great deal of pleasure by himself and for himself. The camera becomes an extension of the person. It precludes having to make conversation. Harvey decided this time gave him an excellent opportunity to study and learn more about this field – to learn more about colors, to study flowers and nature, to become expert in taking pictures of animals, and of the landscape.

His ideal was to be like the well-known Vineyard photographer, Alison Shaw. He would carry her bag, or do anything to learn from her. Soon after his retirement, Harvey's wish was granted. He was able to take a week's workshop with Ms. Shaw. He enthused that other than being with Ellie, it was one of the greatest weeks of his life.

Today he has reached a point where he has showings of his photographs, and he cannot believe that people actually pay for his work. It began as a labor of love, and turned into a business that he never envisioned.

Ellie and Harvey were so prepared for the transition to retire that they hardly skipped a beat. They retired in the spring of 2003, sold their condominium in Quincy, and moved bag and baggage to Martha's Vineyard in May. For Harvey, the transition was somewhat difficult: He had to decide which tee-shirt was appropriate for each day! Photography and travel took up about 50 percent of his time. The rest is made up of:

◆ Some accounting clients to help defray the costs of a considerable investment in the photography business

◆ Treasurer of the Democratic Town Committee

◆ Planning Committee work – affordable housing/economic development/conservation and open space

◆ Volunteering for SCORE (Service Core of Retired Excutives), which helps people start and maintain businesses

◆ Puttering in the yard

Ellie did not want a schedule in retirement, since she had been so over-scheduled all her life. She is still doing a multitude of things, but does not feel as pressured. She can turn it on or off as necessary. Here is the laundry list of activities she has gotten herself into in just the short time she has been spending full time on the Island.

- ◆ She is on a committee that is looking into building a new Town Hall and Town Campus. She is willing to do short, defined projects.

- ◆ Helped organize the first Relay For Life for cancer on Martha's Vineyard

- ◆ She and Harvey exercise at a health club to keep healthy.

- ◆ She works 20 hours a week in a retail shop for a 27 year-old woman entrepreneur. Ellie always wanted to work retail, and loves it.

- ◆ Ellie is back involved in music and drama (meets with a play reading group) and church

- ◆ They are both very busy in their own worlds but wouldn't want any less time with each other

- ◆ Being together is their favorite thing.

Ellie and Harvey have always loved to travel, and having more leisure time provides them with this opportunity. They have been traveling for three months out of the 15 since their retirement. A good 20 percent of the time traveling as a couple is great if you love the same things. They gave each other a cross-country trip with very loose timing as a retirement gift.

They moved to Martha's Vineyard in April, and on May 21st went on their first trip. They went to Niagara Falls, Cleveland (to visit the Rock & Roll Hall of Fame), Chicago, Minnesota, the Grand Tetons, Yellowstone National Park and the state of Washington, where they have relatives. They traveled home via Canada and were back by July 2nd.

The next venture was south in the winter. They went to Washington, D.C., Raleigh, Savannah, St. Augustine, Orlando, Naples and New Orleans. This was a three-week trip. Finally, in May they spent three weeks in the southwest ending at a family wedding in Boulder, Colorado, where they met up with yours truly. Ellie says, "Traveling is great, but we don't want to spend too much time away from Martha's Vineyard."

Only weeks ago Ellie had another cancer scare. They had talked about going to Machu Picchu in Peru, and the Galapagos Islands in Equador, but decided they had spent too much money on travel. After a series of tests, the results, thank goodness, were negative. Upon receiving the results, they both looked at each other, and the first words out of Harvey's mouth were, "Let's go on that trip!" so during October/November off they will go to South America. Ellie says, "I don't want to know when I'm going to die – I just want to know how long the money has to last!"

Ellie and Harvey state that, "Finances are extremely important in preparing for retirement. Although you do not necessarily make a ton of money in the public sector, the pensions are adequate, and health benefits are excellent." They are spending a little more money than they expected because of the photography business, however, they are defraying those costs with part-time jobs.

They engaged a financial planner, their friend, Christopher Bean of Merrill Lynch, early in their retirement planning to help them through the process. He convinced them to buy long-term health insurance. There are two sides to this coin, and people should study the alternatives thoroughly. They went from high expenses and relatively high salaries (for government workers), to a pension and low expenses. For the most part it has worked. They are taking part-time jobs for a little more money, but it is very discretionary. They have no debt, no mortgage, and own three cars outright. I think they are in good shape.

Harvey offers, "Don't retire unless you are really convinced that you want to retire. My thought process went something like this: I have a shot at living on an island; I am not going to be accountable for my time; I do not have to work for anybody, and I still have my health and can remain active. It all added up to *I am ready!* However, if you really want to keep going in your regular job – you should. You possibly may want to phase into retirement over time."

"It is all in your frame of mind," Ellie chimes in. "Married women rarely thought about retirement. They would be on their husband's retirement schedule. Not in today's world. Women must plan financially. Women should not plan on leaning on a man. Women must become independent. Even younger women should think 40-50 years out."

When asked about what legacy are they leaving, Harvey said, "I have tried to be true to myself. To really get the most out of life, one must be in touch with themselves. It does not mean being selfish – it just means being caring, loving and charitable. Participate in social reform. Retire because you know it is the right thing to do for you. I touched the lives of a great many people. I hope that I made this place a little better. I hope that I set good standards for my children. I have always asked them to live up to their own expectations – their own potential. Just be a good member of society, and enjoy life and give back something in return."

Ellie's legacy is her children and grandchildren. One of her priorities in retirement is spending more time with them. "I don't think about a personal legacy at all. People are incredibly lucky if they have someone with whom to share their retirement. Whether you are together or you have to go it alone, retirement is not the end – it is the next phase. And there might be a next phase after that. I could end up with another career – who knows?

If, for some reason, Harvey was not here, it could change my life again. I would have to re-evaluate – re-assess. Second marriages are interesting. We are more mature, more introspective. Harvey and I probably would not have gotten together when we were young – we have both changed in a way that brought us together…and we're lovin' it!"

In a nutshell

Ellie and Harvey Beth really are the prototype retirement couple who had a plan and are sticking to it. They are definitely not going to be cheated out of life.

- Ellie and Harvey planned their retirement and had a definite plan in place ten years prior to the actual date.
- They designed a program to bridge their finances from work life to retirement with the help of a professional financial planner.
- Ellie and Harvey built their retirement home in advance.
- They have similar interests, however, each still maintains their own life and involvements.
- Harvey turned his hobby of photography into a retirement business.
- Their passion is traveling, and they have done a great deal of it.
- Ellie transferred her interest on the mainland to volunteerism on Martha's Vineyard.
- They are both vigorous about maintaining their health. They exercise daily.

- Harvey's volunteering includes helping others in business by participating in the SCORE program that helps people open new businesses.

- Ellie always wanted to work in a retail shop, so she spends 20 hours a week in a gift shop – and loves it!

- Ellie maintains that women must become independent, and not plan on leaning on a man. Even younger women should plan 40 to 50 years out.

- Both of our subjects strongly believe in giving back to society.

- Family is very important to both of them. As they get older they are becoming more involved in family activities.

5

A Series of Right Angles

They say one's persona is formed by the time you reach 10 years of age. Hence, who you are by this age is who you are going to be as an adult. If you were fastidious as a youngster, you will be fastidious as an adult; if you were very structured in your youth, you'll be the same as you get older, and so on. Warren Radtke has been on a mission all his life to help his fellowman, and this has manifested itself in a variety of ways throughout his 70 years.

Growing up in Chicago, he watched his enterprising father involved in a multitude of endeavors and emulated his father's work ethic throughout the years. His dad's primary occupation was head of a laboratory as a feed chemist, however, he was also involved with a gas station, restaurant, and a small bowling alley. His stay-at-home mom kept the books for all of these enterprises.

Warren was quite academic, and matriculated at Northwestern University in Evanston, Illinois, where he majored in Finance and Accounting. His father wanted him to follow that path because he felt with a background in accounting and finance he would never be out of work.

Warren's work life, as you will see, has never really ended – and he is not even sure if it had a beginning. The two words that represent the themes that permeate his life are 'helping,' and 'peace.' Some people see Warren's journey as a series of right turns, however, Warren emphatically sees his life's path with the strong threads of these two themes winding through it.

His first job out of school was with General Electric Credit Corporation. He quickly learned how to spot a good credit. They taught him by putting him on the "repo" truck every Saturday. A lot happened in his three-plus years with GE. He worked in seven cities, ran an office in Rockford, Illinois, with a staff of people and the responsibility of $16 million in credit. This was in 1960, when Warren was 25 years old. Also, during this time, he met and married his wife, Judith.

He was interested enough in dealer credit, however, his real interest was in the human problems that small businessmen were dealing with. He found their problems far more interesting than paying their trust receipts. At Northwestern, his favorite two courses were Human Problems in Business Administration, and Production and Personnel. Are you starting to get the picture?

Here comes the first right angle. Warren was always interested in religion, mainly from an academic point of view. He was not a particularly pious man, but found religion profoundly interesting. One day, literally at the church door, an Episcopal parish priest asked Warren if he had ever considered the seminary. Warren asked if you had to sign your name in blood to enter. "No," said the priest. "Then I'll give it a try a year at a time," said Warren.

We will also find that Warren was risk-oriented, curious, and sometimes an impulsive sort of a chap. Both he and his wife had saved money by working additional jobs, so Warren resigned from GE and began to scratch that intellectual itch.

Warren and his wife picked up stakes and ventured off to Boston where he enrolled in the Episcopal Divinity School at Harvard University. This connection with Harvard is a tie that is a strong bond for Warren even to this day. His wife was accepted to Simmons School of Social Work with the ultimate goal of becoming a psychotherapist.

So, they were in a new city, and both working on their graduate degrees at the same time. His was a three-year program, and hers a two-year. After two years, she had her degree, but Warren, with one year to go, was certain he was not going to work in the church, although he had applied to be a candidate for the ministry just to keep his options open. He felt that he might as well finish the last year and at least get the degree.

Every seminary student was placed in a field assignment, and Warren's was as an assistant to the Chaplain at Harvard. His assignment was the prestigious School of Business Administration. Some of the people he met during those years are still friends to this day.

Graduation came, and Warren, who still wasn't completely vested in the idea of making the church his life, took a half-time position with a large Episcopal Church in the greater Detroit area. The other half-time position he took (here comes another right angle) was with the well-known N.T.L. (National Training Laboratories), because he was interested in how adults learn.

NTL was involved in "adult learning theory." The church was interested in those types of things at that time. At NTL, he learned a great deal about consulting, including how to frame questions and how to get information.

The appointment in Michigan was just for one year, and Warren and his young wife had been smitten by Boston and wanted to go back east. Warren really enjoyed certain parts of the work. He loved "hatching, matching and dispatching" – the part of the life cycle involved with parish ministry. He loved being involved with people's lives at meaningful turning points.

While at the seminary, there was a joint program at the Harvard Business School on ethics – where faith and work interact. In Detroit, he became involved with the Detroit Industrial Mission. This program involved clergy working in factories so they could live the plight of their parishioners. He always gravitated to the work and people-problem side of business.

He decided to give his work with in clergy a little more time. "There is work to be done," said Warren. "Just get me to a church that's near Boston." He was hired by a church in Melrose, Massachusetts, a suburb of Boston. A short time into his ministry, the rector of the church retired, and Warren was elected to be his successor. For 16 years, from 1965-1981, he was an Episcopal Priest, Rector of the Church, and had a large staff, both paid and volunteer, that he managed. In the meantime, his wife had a successful psychotherapy practice, and they were raising three children.

Warren did something radical for those days, although he didn't realize it was radical at the time. Because he was interested in the work life of people, he began visiting his parishioners at their place of employment. Thus he began moonlighting, helping workers with their problems, and business owners with their problems. He was in church ministry during the mid-1970s when the area was hit with devastating layoffs.

Warren became acquainted with the renowned author of the book, *What Color is Your Parachute?*, Richard Bolles, who was also an Episcopal Minister. He got tips from Bolles, and realized that he was really very good at helping people sort out where they should go next with their lives. The Bishop said "There are some clergy who shouldn't be in the clergy any more, but I don't know what to do with them." Warren retorted, "I think I can help."

So the Bishop referred the most difficult member of the clergy to Warren, and two weeks later (although honestly with little help from Warren) he had a new job! The Bishop was delighted, and began to send Warren more clergy who needed to make a graceful exit from the church. Soon various parishioners started to hear of these successful stories, and Warren was inundated with requests for help.

Warren also knew the highly successful Bernard Haldane, the dean of the "retail" job counseling service, and also an Episcopal layperson. At this point, all things pointed in the direction of creating a job counseling practice.

Warren decided to open an office one day a week in downtown Boston where he charged a nominal fee for his service. This was during 1979 and 1980. He had been in the ministry much longer than he ever would have imagined, and it was time to reassess his own life and career, and begin to do more of what he liked to do and less of what he didn't like to do. He went to the Bishop and revealed his plan. The Bishop blessed Warren's decision and said it would be a terrific ministry for him. He graciously let Warren keep his ties to the church, including his pension, etc.

Here's the next right angle. Warren went to 24 Federal Street in Boston (the old Eaton Vance building), rented an office, borrowed some furniture, got call waiting for the telephone, and voila, was in business as a sole practitioner. He decided the best firms to call on were banks and insurance companies because they were paternalistic and people-intensive organizations. Warren wasn't interested in hi-tech. This was 1981, and the concept of "outplacement," i.e., helping people who had been laid off, was in its infancy. Companies paid the fee, and Warren was helping his fellowman.

The thread continues. We knew that Warren would be terrific in the counseling end of the business, but could he be successful on the sales and marketing side? Wait a minute! I forgot to tell you that as a kid he always won the prize for selling the most magazines, and won the bike for delivering the most papers on his paper route. And didn't we say you are who you are when you are 10? Was there any doubt that he would be successful? Not in the least. With all those Harvard contacts, and wider church contacts, and his parishioners pulling for him, along with his nerve and get up and go. It was a mix just made for success.

He was in business for just a short time when he got a phone call from a fellow in Connecticut which would change his life forever. The man, named Boardman Thompson, said, "My minister knows you and he says that you won't cheat me. I am working outplacement business with Pan American World Airways and they have six people in Boston to be counseled. Can you help them?" Warren said, "of course." They were brief interventions. Pan Am was happy, the candidates were happy, and Boardman Thompson was happy.

Thompson called soon thereafter and stated that a few guys were putting together a larger outplacement company. He asked if Warren would be interested. Warren said, "Sure, I'll listen." He went to New York and met four guys named Lochheim, Evans, Fish and Thompson (LEFT). Warren agreed to be part of the group, but said, "We can't call it LEFT Associates! Let's use my first initial "R" and call it Right Management."

That was in 1981, and 24 years later Right Management is one of the largest and most successful worldwide publicly traded companies in existence. Ultimately, as Executive Vice President, Warren was responsible for the eastern third of the U.S., which translated to 60 percent of the revenue. But in 1995, Warren felt it was time to make the break.

However one more success by one of his people kept him in the fold into the next year. One of Warren's people won the job of downsizing one-third of Pepsi International Worldwide's workforce. Warren took an office in London and worked the areas of India, Pakistan, the Middle East, and Africa. The deal put two cents on the bottom line and was one of the most successful outplacement ventures in the history of the business. It was a nice ending to a great career. Did I say ending? Shame on me; I should know better. Let's see where this enterprising fellow takes us next!

Warren "retired" on March 1, 1996. That same day he walked over to a boatyard in Boston harbor and got the Sea-Tow franchise for Portland, Maine. This is basically AAA on water. He went into this business venture with his son, who is a high school teacher in Falmouth, Maine, and who has the summers off. They incorporated as the Marine Maine Group. Warren got his Coast Guard license and felt it was a nice way to also bond with his son. Now, 19 years later, he spends maybe a day a month in the venture. It's never been a real money maker, but the intangible value is worth more than money.

Warren has never stopped helping people. While his non-compete contract was in force, he helped people *pro bono*. After his contract was completed he still received calls to help. So, he's come full circle and still does some counseling for some prestigious senior counseling firms. And, oh yes, he is doing work for the vocationally troubled alumni at guess where? You got it – Harvard Business School. The old ties are still in play. That should be enough to keep our friend Warren busy, right? Wrong! Take a look at what else is on his "retirement" plate along with some of his volunteer involvements throughout the years:

- ◆ Involved in civil rights movement

- ◆ Registered voters in Montgomery, Alabama

- ◆ Involved with anti-war movement during Vietnam War

- ◆ Currently involved with Palestinian-Israeli relationship – Peace and Justice – travels there annually with a mission

- ◆ Huntington Theatre – Trustee Emeritus

- ◆ Clergy Wellness Project – designs curriculum for vocational wellness

- ◆ His wife wound down her practice; studied to be a mid-wife; founded an NGO (non-governmental organization) called the Circle of Women in Mexico – a micro-economic project helping women in the weaving industry. She runs a birthing clinic, and Warren is her administrative assistant. They travel to Mexico many times a year.

Warren and his wife, Judith, have three very successful children. The oldest son lives in New York, was a Rhodes Scholar, and has a Doctorate from Oxford and is the Senior Vice President of the Asia Society (involved with Political and Economic Programming). The other children, are boy-girl twins, with the daughter living in Brookline, Massachusetts. She is the Director of Philanthropic Services for the Boston Foundation. The other son is a high school social studies teacher in Falmouth, Maine, Chairman of the Portland School Committee, and an owner of the Sea-Tow business with his dad.

I asked Warren if he had ever failed. He gave a long, pregnant pause and said, "I've never crashed and burned, but I have had an occasional hiccup once in a while." The only thing he would have done differently was to spend a little less time in parish work.

He then went on to say that the thread has always been helping people. "I'm always in the process of learning something. I had to teach myself the outplacement business. I had to teach myself the Sea-Tow business. All along life's journey people make decisions about where their money is going to come from, and how will they spend their time. This is specifically relevant in retirement. I'm just trying to make a contribution.

"All my life I've always been in charge of my own time. Nobody checked me in and nobody checked me out. I like it that way. I have a number of streams of income and have it professionally managed. I've been pretty healthy. I had a heart incident about 15 years ago – very minor, and I stopped smoking before I was 50. I tend to watch my weight.

"I've always been opportunistic and very curious," he continues, "but a great deal has been by the seat-of-my-pants. My primary skill was that I learned to be a good listener. I'm relatively bright, a quick read, a risk taker, and I'm not afraid to try something new. It's important for everyone to think of their work life as a portfolio. Charles Handy introduced this concept in his book, *The Age of Reason*,

- ◆ Some work you do for wages
- ◆ Some work you do for a fee
- ◆ Some work you do for yourself
- ◆ Some work you call education
- ◆ Some work you give away

"At all stages of our life we should be looking at our portfolio to gauge whether or not it is out of balance. Look at balancing your work portfolio just as you have to balance and rebalance your financial portfolio from time to time," advises Warren.

Thus ended my visit with Warren Radtke. I can assure you that if we chat with Warren ten years from now, he will be chock full of new ventures and exciting stories. Retirement? No, I don't think so. Just the next phase of a very busy and successful life.

In a nutshell

Those devilish eyes give him away. He does things out of the goodness of his heart. He and his wife will be giving to others until their dying breath.

- Warren knew when to retire and went out with a flourish.

- He was never afraid to follow his heart and his passion.

- Caring and giving were his watchwords.

- He and his wife, Judith, were always risk-oriented. They never shied away from doing something outside the box.

- Warren retired one day and immediately moved to the next phase of his life to a profession completely foreign to the one he had just left: the assistance towing industry.

- Gregarious and outgoing, people gravitated to him for advice and counsel.

- Warren was always curious and very opportunistic. He was smart, a good listener, and a terrific businessman.

- He married a woman with similar values. In retirement they're helping with development, health care, and literacy in Mexico. Their life's mission of helping people is never ending.

- Warren does not view retirement as "retirement," but rather as simply a new phase with a re-balanced portfolio of work.

6

From Hi-Tech
to High-Flies

Gene Brundage grew up in the shadow of the Polo Grounds in New York, the former home of the San Francisco Giants. His family were avid New York Giants fans, and took young Gene to as many Giants games as they could. But more about that later.

Gene matriculated at Marquette University in Milwaukee, Wisconsin, earning a degree in Engineering. At age 29, Gene joined Raytheon Corporation where he enjoyed 37 years of success, and continued to progress up the ranks in Program Management. He worked in the Government Equipment Division, Missile Systems Division, and in Satellite Communications. His technical areas of expertise were in Hardware and Software Design and Test, along with Software and Hardware Integration for the Navy Satellite Communications System.

The Brundages settled in Framingham, Massachusetts, where they began to raise a family. Gene was fascinated by the form of government in the town, so in 1960 he ran for and was elected as a Town Meeting

Member in a representative town meeting form of government. He served with distinction in that capacity until 1992, when after 32 years, he was appointed to the Finance Committee.

The Finance Committee is the most influential town committee in Framingham. It is charged with the responsibility of considering any and all municipal questions that it deems appropriate. It has the authority to investigate the books, accounts, and management of any department of the Town. Gene has gravitated toward two specific areas within the town in his Finance Committee capacity. They are Public Safety, and because of his software background, the IT (Information Technology) world.

When I asked Gene how he prepared for retirement, he stated he was lax in that area. He didn't plan or devote much time to thinking what he would do after leaving Raytheon. Sure, he had his 401(k) and Raytheon Pension Program, so he felt confidant he would be financially okay (who ever thought that 2000-2003 would bring stock market disaster via a recession?), but as far as how he would fill his time, he never gave it a thought. (By the way, as you will see, this is a thread that runs throughout this book.)

At age 66, Gene was still going strong when he shattered his ankle in three places when he slipped on the ice. He was on the shelf for the next six weeks. After a period of rehab, Gene returned to Raytheon, but it was never the same. He was closing in on age 67 and also had just been diagnosed as a Type 2 diabetic. He stayed about six more months, then finally put the cap on an illustrious 37-year career.

Retirement was at hand. He had some ideas of how to fill his time in retirement, but nothing in depth. But transition from the work-a-day world to retirement was easy. Once done, he never had a desire to return to the 40 hour-a-week grind ever again – even on a consulting basis.

It's been ten years into retirement and the "honey-do" list that his wife drew up upon his ending work is still hanging on the wall. "A homeowner knows there is always work to do around the house," said Gene. "I haven't gotten around to doing any of it yet. If you came around to my place you would see what I mean!"

Part of the recovery process for that shattered ankle was to strengthen it with exercise. And of course the same holds true for one who is diabetic. As a matter of fact, exercise seems to be the therapy of choice for a lot of ills.

Just about this time, Gene applied for more life insurance, but he was turned down, mainly because of the diabetes. Well, Gene was not to be thwarted. He was going to take charge and get control over his physical problems. He started to formulate some plans: retire, exercise and lose weight. He thought "out of the box" and reminisced of his childhood when he would long to go to those baseball games he loved so much. "Why not?" he thought. "It's worth a shot. The worst they can say is no. It doesn't cost anything to ask." Okay, Gene, go for it!

So, only a few months after he retired in February 1994, Gene drove down Yawkey Way in Boston, stepped inside Fenway Park, and asked for an application to become a 66 year-old rookie usher. And lo and behold, two months later, he got a call asking him if he was still interested and could he work opening day.

Gene was ecstatic; it was a dream come true. He would walk up and down the stairs strengthening his ankle and reducing his blood sugar numbers, and of course be able to sneak a peek at his all-time favorite sport – baseball. It was as if he had died and woken up in heaven.

So opening day of the 1994 season, 66 year-old Gene Brundage was fitted for a uniform, given an orientation, and sent to where all rookies start in this business – the bleachers.

In ten years, Gene has seen it all. He has worked his way around the ballpark, was promoted to the right field grandstand, the left field wall area near "The Green Monster," and now is working behind the visitor's dugout in section 25. It's a very personal business: the rag that wipes off your seat comes from the usher's home – not from the Red Sox. You can't get much more personal than that. I guess if you can't find a rag, you'd have to call in sick!

Ushers are required to be at the park two and one-half hours before the game and are paid a "game rate." The job keeps you young, as you are constantly interfacing with people. Weekend nights can be a challenge as the beer flows. Saturday and Sunday afternoons seem to be the easiest, with families predominating the crowd.

There have been hundreds of funny happenings over the years, but Gene recounts two that stand out. One year at the trade day deadline of July 31st, a woman held up a sign saying, *I'd like to trade my husband for #7, Trot Nixon.* Gene went over to the woman with his condolences and said, "I am truly sorry ma'am. It's eight p.m. and the trade deadline was at three p.m. this afternoon." The woman was quite disappointed!

The great Ricky Henderson was playing left field for Oakland. A fan hanging over the wall in the left field grandstand was heckling Ricky and using profane language to boot. Ricky came into the dugout and complained to the police. They sent a cop up, and along with security, had the fan removed. Somehow, an inning later, the fan reappeared and started heckling Ricky again. This time he was arrested for trespassing, and when they ran his name through the computer they found that he had outstanding warrants. So Ricky in essence made a pinch at the ballpark, and Gene indirectly had a hand in it.

On Patriots Day 1999, Gene had a heart attack just before the game. Fortunately they had EMTs and a defibrillator at the park that brought him back. He was rushed to Beth Israel Hospital, where they put a stent in the one blocked artery, and six weeks later tough Gene was back at his post (quicker than Nomar and Trot!). His cardiologist calls him the Poster Child for all of his ills that he has had to deal with and has overcome. His ankle, then diabetes, and now his heart…plus losing 40 lbs. A determined man, that Gene Brundage!

"What about the future?" I asked Gene "Well, I really want to stay with the Red Sox," he replied. "We are on a mission – I kinda have to stay until we win it all." Which finally happened in 2004!

"And I love my Finance Committee work," he said. "I'm also involved with Cardiac Rehab three mornings a week, where I ride the bike and walk the treadmill. I've met some terrific people there. The jokes fly – we have a good time – they are a fantastic group of men and women. I've met a lot of people whom we have socialized with outside of rehab.

"Retirement has really been a plus for me. I honestly can't say enough about retirement. My wife and I bought a two-week time-share in Mexico and have traded it for weeks both in the U.S. and throughout Europe. We love to travel. We have curbed our foreign travel lately, unfortunately, due to the terror threats. However, hopefully as the threat eases, we will resume our foreign adventures.

"I do regret not devoting more time to planning for my retirement. My planning was, in a word, "weak." I'd advise people to plan more, especially with the potential demise of Social Security. You will need more of your own funds to beat inflation. To keep our minds active, both my wife and I do at least one crossword puzzle a day. And I read a lot of books. I also teach mathematics to gifted fourth grade children two mornings a week.

"We had a one-day seminar about retirement at my company. It did have some value, but not nearly enough. Companies have a responsibility to prepare their employees, both financially and mentally, about the challenge that may face them in retirement. It can be a shock to the system.

"I've always had a yearning to learn. In the late '50s, as a veteran with G. I. Bill privileges, I was able to take courses at Framingham State College tuition free. With that opportunity I received a Master of Arts degree in International Marketing. I'm not sure how much it helped me at Raytheon, but I really felt good about gaining that additional degree. Seniors can take tuition free courses. You can never have enough education.

I subscribe to getting out of the house, going to school, meeting younger people, interfacing with those people, and keeping your mind working. You'll get something out of it and live longer. Activities for seniors are exploding. Travel to time shares across the whole world is at your fingertips. My last word of advice is to think more about retirement before the fact."

Well, Gene, for a guy who really didn't plan, you've had a great run in your first ten years of retirement. We wish you many more active and productive years.

And go get 'em Sox!

 In a nutshell

Approaching 80 years of age, Gene looks at life like a wide-eyed kid. The little boy in him shines through when he talks about his Red Sox.

- He took his passion for baseball and created the next phase in his retirement with a job as an usher at Fenway Park, Boston.

- Gene laments not planning early enough for retirement.

- He volunteers in schools utilizing his technical skills working with youngsters.

- He and his wife love to travel. They have found time shares a very inexpensive way to go.

- Gene and his wife find time to complete a crossword puzzle every day to keep their minds active.

- He is heavily invested in his town's activities by serving on the prestigious Finance Committee.

- Exercise is key to maintaining his health. Walking up and down the aisles at Fenway Park provides a lot of exercise that helps in addressing his health problems.

- Gene continues to make new friends. He turned his thrice-weekly visits to cardiac rehab into a social experience.

- Gene takes advantage of the many educational courses offered for seniors to provide the opportunity to interface with young people, while broadening his horizons.

7

A Full Part-Time Job

When you drive out of the Pittsburgh Airport you must take either a left or a right. Right takes you to downtown Pittsburgh, left leads to the lovely suburb of Sewickley, where our subject, Nancy Rogoff, spent her youth.

Early on she had a desire to be her own person, along with an insatiable wanderlust. Neither Sewickley, nor even Pittsburgh, were big or active enough for this gregarious young woman, so she gravitated to the more "hip" city of Boston for her college years, graduating from Boston University School of Education in 1972 with a degree in Elementary Education.

She always wanted to teach, and loved working with young people. So she truly thought teaching was her calling. However, like many plans, it was not meant to be – at least at this time of her life. Her graduation coincided with the advent of a new Educational Reform Act in Massachusetts entitled Chapter 766, and even though many new teachers were being hired, they all were being designated to the special needs area. This was not Nancy's thing, so she had to go to plan B. (One always needs a plan B, whether in work or retirement life.)

Plan B was a Band-Aid of sorts while she decided which direction to take. She opted to work at a stock brokerage firm as a secretary to several salespeople. All of the salesmen were of a single gender, which was the rule in those days. Watching this activity every day lured her into the sales game. She thought, "I can do that. I can be just as good as these guys."

But, since her strength was working with people and not stocks and bonds, she decided to "sell people." She decided to go into the employment agency business where she could use her skills and outgoing nature to match individuals with jobs. She was an instant success. Her concentration was in the placement of key-punch operators in what is known today as the IT (Information Technology) area. Little did she know she was entering the wonderful world of Human Resources. In those days we knew it as Industrial Relations and then later as Personnel.

As Affirmative Action came into play with various corporations, more opportunities were being unearthed for women. Nancy, who had spent the last few years interfacing with many Greater Boston corporations, decided it was time to switch over to the corporate side and ply her trade in the direct world, as opposed to the third party or consulting side.

She was hired as a Personnel Assistant at a small communications company. It was the classic entry-level, non-exempt job that included staffing, compensation, and benefits, along with counseling. Any and all activities assumed by the personnel department were fair game. It was a great training ground. It was seat-of-the-pants on-the-job training. It was a trial by fire, and a great learning experience.

The next step up the ladder was to move to an exempt professional recruiter's position, hiring engineers and the like. This she did at a company called Kollsman Instruments in Merrimack, New Hampshire. The only catch was that she lived in Newton, Massachusetts, a commute of 50 miles each way. She was caught on the road during the infamous blizzard of '78 and that soured her on such a long commute.

Her restless and ever-searching nature led her to take another risk. Why not? She and her friend had been talking about it for a while. She would keep the Kollsman job, but get into her own business as well. She would do both. So, she and her friend took the plunge and opened a Laundromat in the Cleveland Circle area of Boston. They borrowed the money and studied the inner workings and just did it!

But again, it wasn't enough action for our risk-taking, put-a-toe-in-the-water Nancy. As the Laundromat became self-sufficient, she needed more action. Her question was, "Where do I go from here?" Nancy went to a human resources placement firm to attempt to reach the next highest level on the corporate ladder and discovered a new option to consider. It was suggested she become a contract recruiter. "What is that?" she asked.

A contract recruiter is an expert that is placed in a company on a temporary basis to help out for a period of time when there is a large hiring need. They are paid hourly and must assimilate into the program quickly, as the need is usually critical. Once the need subsides, the contractor leaves and goes to another assignment in another company. There is always action, and you are the expert in the staffing arena.

This suited Nancy just fine. It worked for her personality and her trigger-action mind. Her first assignment was at the Polaroid Corporation in their Battery Division, where she hired quality assurance and manufacturing people.

The next assignment took her to Digital Equipment Corporation's Central Engineering Division, where she was the first hi-tech woman to recruit among mostly male engineers. Being a contractor taught her how to be a consultant as an inside person and rev up very quickly.

Thinking retrospectively, Nancy says that she never thought that Digital would take a chance on a female non-engineer. "I guess we both took a risk!" she said. "But I've never been afraid to take a risk. It's fun to try things that you haven't done before, and see if you can conquer and succeed. It's important to grasp your dreams and keep raising the bar, because you only go around once."

She was so successful in her first six months as a contractor that Digital offered her a full-time, permanent employee position. Nancy spent a total of five years at DEC in Engineering and Digital Research, where the assignments were cutting, leading edge, and all different. At that point Digital was an exciting place to work.

"My world was staffing," said Nancy, "but I was allowed to venture far from the norm. I built a recruiting van just to take to college campuses. We recruited in the greater Detroit area when the auto industry was in its doldrums. We could be as creative as we could be."

It was the perfect match for a woman who wanted to be the first and do it all with few strings attached.

Finding a Full Part-Time Job

"When did it change?" she asks. "I guess when I became a mom. This was another big risk, because it changed my priorities. Travel, plus long hours in the recruiting world for a "hot" company led to not being able to see my baby. I made the conscious decision that I just had to adjust. My family became my priority. I had built a good reputation as a hi-tech recruiter, so I decided to go back into contracting – but under my own terms. I would control my working hours. Since I was paid by the hour, if I had to be home for any reason, I just wouldn't be paid. It took away the guilt," said Nancy.

Nancy established guidelines very early. She only worked three to four days a week. She felt there was a lot of wasted time in the average work week anyway. She would just do the job, and thought she should be able to complete the assignments in less than a "normal" work week.

It worked very efficiently. So it wasn't necessarily retirement, but it was a work adjustment. I guess you would call it a very full part-time job.

"While my daughter was growing up," said Nancy, "my main outside activity was being involved in her school activities, i.e., PTA, school outings, religious school, athletic events, and helping her with her homework. At the same time, I maintained my three to four day a week recruiting consulting practice. I didn't have the bandwidth to do all the outside activities that I would have liked to do.

"Along with my husband, who is a dentist, I also helped raise two step-children through college, marriages, and the like. It was virtually impossible to participate in many outside activities. The only groups that I joined were professional human resources societies to help further my career and to network. Without family in the area to help and support me, I was truly on my own."

"I'm not sure when my status changed," said Nancy, "but with the workforce getting younger and me getting older, I began to realize that, as I reached my early 50s, I would have to begin making a transition. I discussed various options with my husband about retiring, semi-retiring, or at least doing it differently. I believe that we have three or four careers in our lifetime, either paid or unpaid, and retirement is the evolution of exactly that."

I asked Nancy about the financial impact of losing her income. Her answer was that when you bring up three children, there are tremendous expenses. After the children are essentially gone, the expense line diminishes appreciably. "With the house paid off, the financial impact will be minimal," she said. "Now our expenses are under control. It will not be quite as devastating as it would have been ten years ago."

There comes a time when outside influences dictate that it's time to slow down. Nancy has had two back operations over the past few years. So you have to listen to your body. She also lost both her parents within a six month period. She realized that there is only so much time out there, and you have to go for it.

Well, the kids are pretty much gone, finances are in good shape, and Nancy admits she is in some form of retirement. I guess it's time to sit out on the deck, with her feet up sipping a Cosmopolitan. Or as the *Sex In The City* ladies call it, "sipping a Cosmo." *Buzz, wrong answer!* When I asked Nancy what she was doing to keep busy, I got a whole next chapter of this risk-oriented busy lady's life.

Never one to sit idle, here is how she is filling her time in what we will tongue-in-cheek call retirement. She is not being paid, so in that vein it's retirement from a paid occupation, but wait until you hear Nancy's schedule. Take notes – it's a menu of activities that she never had time to do, and that some of you just might want to get involved with.

Dogs have always been Nancy's passion. She has two Golden Retrievers, Bailey and Madison, and has become a volunteer for the Golden Retriever Rescue League. Her responsibility is to visit the homes of potential adopters. She interviews families to determine whether or not they are appropriate to adopt a rescue dog. She takes one of her dogs along with her, and is having a blast doing it.

She attended a full-day training session where they provided her with several interview questions. But, who better to conduct an interview than Nancy? Some of her reports were so good they were incorporated into the training program.

One funny story tells about her visit to a potential adoptive family. She asked the five year-old son if he was excited by the possibility of having a dog. "No, I hate dogs!" he exclaimed. That family did not qualify.

She always had a desire to explore her creative arts side. So, she took a watercolor course and realized she didn't know how to paint. Next in line was a drawing class at the DeCordova Museum in Lincoln, Massachusetts, where she realized she also couldn't draw. Undaunted, she now is enrolled in a ceramics class, and is loving it. Outside of the proverbial ashtrays ("nobody smokes in my house") she has made an exquisite flower vase for show. It's a three-hour weekly class. Nancy says it's fun building with your hands and thinking of things to create.

Keeping fit is almost like a religion with Nancy. She has been able to do her exercise routine three times a week at a local gym without the stress of time constraints. She has also added a class on yoga, which not only helps her twice-operated back, but also lifts her spiritually.

A firm believer in giving back because she feels blessed and so fortunate in life, Nancy is part of the Boston Literacy Program, which promotes reading in urban schools. Nancy spends time each week tutoring a third grader in West Roxbury whose parents do not speak English. She also volunteers for the Newton Food Pantry, where she delivers food to a Spanish family who does not speak English and who has many children.

Traveling has been one of Nancy's primary goals. She has an insatiable appetite to learn, to see, and to experience new things and interesting places. She's traveled extensively to Africa, Europe, South America and Israel, along with quite a bit of domestic sightseeing. One needs to maintain good health and not be afraid to take some travel risks.

So you see in retirement (or whatever it's called), Nancy remains extremely active doing the things she wants to do. "In transition from the working life," says Nancy, "you go to a life where you have to create your own activities. You don't have the luxury of the structure that you had before, so your time allotments are very different." Having all these activities puts Nancy in a structure with which she is quite comfortable.

"One thing that happens at this stage of our lives," says Nancy, "is that we are in the 'club sandwich years.' We are still heavily involved with our children, but have the added responsibility (if we are fortunate enough) of taking care of our elderly parents. These are all-consuming activities. It is quite enlightening. One needs a great many resources and help to deal with both sides of the coin.

"We are living longer and healthier lives, and so we have to do much more preparation for our last 20-30 years. Consider going back to school to recreate yourself. We can make a better effort at helping each other and considering retirees as mentors. Volunteering with the transferable skill sets acquired throughout one's life is a very satisfying way to spend your twilight years."

Legacy Building

"My daughter is my legacy," says Nancy. "She is able to grasp opportunities and be her own person. She is a strong young woman who feels good about who she is and where she is going. I feel that that is what we can do for our children. Set them on the right course in life.

"Oh it would have been nice to have known way back when what I know now, so there wouldn't have been so many bumps in the road. A lot was done by the seat-of-my-pants. I think the kids of today have a lot more opportunity to research their future careers than their parents had. I just fell into Human Resources.

"Would I have done it differently? I guess not. I'm pretty happy. It's been quite a ride and who knows what's next? I'm game for anything."

You always were, Nancy.

 ## In a nutshell

Nancy has never been afraid to try anything. She embraces everything with tremendous enthusiasm, and is busier in retirement than she's ever been.

- Nancy has always been a risk-taker and enjoys doing things out of the box.

- She has energy to burn, and sometimes tends to overdo and not know when she is taking on too much.

- Nancy has many hobbies and interests that were pushed into the background during her formidable work years. They have now moved front and center, as she presently has the time to embrace her passions and interests.

- Volunteering as a Supervisor in the Golden Retriever Rescue League has become the centerpiece of her life. Combined with dog grooming and owning two dogs of her own, she is surrounded with doggie activities.

- With a broad time limit, she and her husband are now able to travel and vacation more freely.

- Nancy has a love of the Arts, and she attends many performances, and has taken several courses associated with this interest.

- Fitness is important to her. She actively works out several times a week, and she tries to take good care of herself.

- Nancy stays in contact with many friends by going to lunch and dinner on an ongoing basis.

- If her schedule is not full, she feels cheated. She wants to do it all!

8

Three Strikes and You're Out?

As a former professional baseball player, 65 year-old Steve Ryder constantly is amazed, as he continues to count his blessings. He has not strayed too far from his Framingham, Massachusetts roots over the years, except for the five years he spent in the Milwaukee (now Atlanta) Braves baseball organization.

The dichotomy of being a superbly conditioned athlete and having many medical problems over the years makes Steve's story a unique one.

The only flag in Steve's young life was a spinal fusion operation at age 13. Other than that, he was a normal teenager and an outstanding youth and high school athlete. He had the normal teenage jobs working for the local Parks & Recreation and School Departments during the summers. After high school, Steve ventured to the University of Massachusetts in Amherst for a year, but the lure of signing a professional baseball contract was just too much.

His decision was between the Phillies and the Braves. After some deliberation, in May of 1958, he signed a contract with the Milwaukee

Braves with a bonus of $30,000. (Steve says he would love to be able to convert that money into today's dollars.)

Here's a kid, only 19 years-old, who had never really been too far from home, and his first assignment was in Eau Claire, Wisconsin for the Northern League. Working in the Northern League is equivalent to playing "A" ball. His two years there were quite an eye-opener for young Ryder.

He met a melting pot of people from all races, creeds and religions. There was a strong influx of "Islanders," even in those days – players from the Dominican Republic, Puerto Rico and Cuba dotted the roster. The players from Cuba were particularly interesting because they were under the Batista regime and were eager for Fidel Castro to take over. Little did they know they had more freedom under Batista than they eventually would have under Castro. Over the years, Castro restricted the activities of Cuban players to playing only for the national team, depriving them of U.S. professional careers.

The other eye-opener was the way African-Americans were treated in the South prior to the 1964 Civil Rights Act. Separate facilities were a shocking indignation to Steve, and something he never witnessed during his life up North.

He remembers playing a game in West Palm Beach, Florida where the white players stayed in a beautiful hotel, and the black players were picked up by a van and transported to "Colored Town." One day Steve, another white teammate, and Hank Aaron's brother, Tommy, a black teammate, stopped at a Howard Johnson's restaurant down south. Tommy said he wasn't hungry and stayed in the car. Steve later learned the reason Tommy said he wasn't hungry was because he was not welcome in that restaurant.

Even the southern white players had an edge to them as they still seemed to be battling the Civil War. This whole experience was quite uncomfortable and unnerving for this sensitive 20 year-old. These were some of life's lessons that the boy from Framingham would never forget.

In 1960, Steve had done well enough to earn a promotion to Cedar Rapids, Iowa, which was comparable to "AA" level baseball. But in June of 1960, his good fortune turned bad. He had a collision with another player and tore the patella from his kneecap. He was on the disabled list for the remainder of the year.

He came back to Cedar Rapids in 1961, but the year was far from his best. His knee injury became a major factor. This outfielder was not a speed demon to begin with, but the knee injury reduced his speed even more.

In 1962, Steve was sent to Yakima, Washington, where he batted fourth (cleanup) and was a fixture against both left- and right-handed pitchers. As a matter of fact, future big-leaguer, Rico Carty, batted fifth in that line-up.

Steve thought he was doing very well, however, by mid-May management brought in a speedier replacement, and they approached Steve to send him to a lower level. Steve was shocked, surprised, and disappointed. He asked for, and was granted, his release from the Braves.

He then got an offer from the New York Mets to go to the California League, but, after careful deliberation, Steve decided the writing was on the wall, that it didn't make sense to continue in baseball, and that he better get on with his life.

Remember the $30,000 bonus money? Well, in the interim during his five years of professional baseball, Steve invested $25,000 of that with his father, who was an independent trucker at the time. With Steve's money, plus his own resources, Steve's father opened up Ryder Concrete, a ready-mix concrete plant in Milford, New Hampshire.

At the same time, Steve felt he needed to obtain his college degree. So he and his new bride moved to Milford, where Steve enrolled at St. Anselms College. Margi taught school, and Steve helped his dad run the business. This worked fine for a while. Steve graduated with a degree in History with a teaching certification. The business was running well with his dad at the helm, so Steve decided he would do what he really wanted to do – teaching and coaching.

His first job was at Marian High School, a small Catholic private school in Framingham, Massachusetts, where he taught and coached baseball, basketball, and football as an assistant. Natick, Massachusetts, was next. The school here had better benefits for his growing family. He spent three years at Coolidge Junior High School, while coaching freshmen baseball and basketball.

In 1969, he coached at Framingham State College, while getting his Master's degree, and was offered the Athletic Director's position in 1970. That began a 35-year love affair with the college that continues to this day. He stayed in this position until 1975, coaching baseball and creating the football and hockey programs. But resources were sparse, and in 1975, Steve decided to rejoin his father to expand the concrete business into sand and gravel operations, along with real estate development.

Steve's father passed away in 1979. The business, plus the responsibility of taking care of his mother, three sisters, and his family, all fell on Steve's shoulders. Other than the spinal fusion as a kid, Steve had been the picture of health. Then, in 1980, at 40 years-old, Steve's life took an alarming turn.

While running the conglomerate in New Hampshire, Steve was shocked to learn in February, after a series of tests, that his heart was in terrible shape. He needed to have quintuple by-pass surgery. The symptoms were minimal, however, he was told that even the mildest exertion could be fatal.

The economy was in trouble, business had tailed off, and the stress level was quite high. This all added up to the condition in which Steve found himself. He certainly hadn't prepared for this eventuality. He never expected to have to slow down at 40 years of age.

Steve never planned for retirement or even semi-retirement – it just came naturally with health issues. This was quite a wake-up call. He had never given it a thought, but now he realized he was vulnerable – a mortal man. He seemed to be recovering nicely, when in May of 1980, only three months after the by-pass surgery, while doing some follow-up treadmill tests in the hospital, he almost died. Steve actually flat-lined for 55 seconds and was revived by shots of lidocaine and the use of paddles.

Two major scares and a slow recovery at 40 years of age changed Steve's life forever. For the next several years, he ran the company, but at a much more relaxed pace. In 1987, due to circumstances beyond his control, Steve closed the company.

At the same time, he began experiencing similar health problems as those seven years before. The surgeons operated again, and this time they performed a double by-pass operation. They wanted to do more, however, his heart was in such bad shape they could only do the two procedures. Undaunted, Steve would not let this get him down. He re-connected with Framingham State College. He never thought of totally stopping – he just had to make an adjustment.

In 1988, he again took on an assignment at the college, this time as an academic advisor. He worked with a variety of students helping them design academic curriculums, change their careers, and obtain Master's Degrees. Steve worked with people from 19 to 70 years of age, and loved it. He was immensely successful because of his diversified background. He made the adjustment to a 20 hour a week part-time job where he is imparting his knowledge and helping people achieve their goals. It's been 16 years, and he is still going strong. There is no quit in Steve Ryder.

Through his life Steve has always been involved in activities outside work. He was the recipient of the coveted Salute to Framingham Award, emblematic of people who have contributed to the well-being of Framingham youngsters. This prestigious award recognizes recipients for their activities and support, which ensures the continued vitality of the community for generations to come. Events such as Nights for Peter Taglienetti (Stanley Cup Hockey Champion), Lou Merloni (Red Sox hometown player), and Salute to Framingham are things that Steve enjoys. He has been quite active in supporting political candidates, as much for the education as for anything else. He has always been a tireless worker for causes in which he believes.

Let's check in on that bad heart again. After by-pass surgery in 1987, things went well for eight years. Then, in 1995, the bottom fell out. His condition deteriorated terribly. He couldn't walk up a flight of stairs. The slightest activity would create tremendous tightness in his chest. Sleeping at night was virtually impossible. So the only option was a heart transplant.

Steve was put on the transplant list on March 17, 1997. Seven months later, he received the transplant, which saved his life. When the damaged heart was removed, it had only one open artery. The doctor claimed not many miles were left on that organ. The transplant was a success, however, the recovery created both physical demands and emotional issues.

Steve eventually recovered completely and decided to slowly get back into selected activities, while returning to his 20 hour a week stint at Framingham State. I told you there are no "three strikes and you're out" with this warrior. The transplant, and the ramifications thereof, changed Steve's thinking forever. No more stressful situations, no more President & CEO of companies – it was time to pick and choose his involvements. He said, "To maintain a quality of life, I had to adjust."

Physical activity was cut way back, he became more selective, but he still participated. After two by-pass operations and a heart transplant he learned he was mortal, but by the same token he didn't want to stop living. "I did stop living at one time, but I had too much time to think and I got very depressed," Steve said.

"The transplant was seven years ago and I'm still doing academic advising. The college has been very supportive. A transplant is a team event. Not only are the surgeons involved, but you must have a stable family life, because you will need a support system beyond the transplant in order for it to be successful.

"Social workers and psychiatrists are part of this team. They try to determine if you will be strong enough emotionally to maintain a life-long regimen of life protecting drugs and medication, while still maintaining some semblance of productivity.

"I've enjoyed every aspect of my life," says Steve. "I consider myself extremely fortunate in two respects: First, when I was 13 years-old, I had a spinal fusion operation. If I had been bumped in a certain way I would have ended up in a wheelchair for the rest of my life. This didn't happen, and I was able to do everything I wanted to do in life. Secondly, the transplant I underwent in 1997 has given me at least seven years to do what I want.

"I was also fortunate in being able to guide my mother through her last years until her passing. This was very important to me, since we were very close. And my involvement with my father in business ensured the financial well-being of all of my family."

Legacy

"I've had a great life, a great run, doing what I wanted," said Steve. "We have four grandchildren who are involved in sports and other activities. I take a great deal of pride and pleasure in them. I'd like to be remembered as someone who was a good person, who never took advantage of anyone, and who tried where he could to help.

"It's good to think about retirement ahead of time, for it comes upon you so fast. You can't sit back and do nothing. Even with a new heart, I know it won't last forever, but I want to get the most out of it while I can.

"It's easy to lose relationships with people when you get out of the mainstream. It's fun to see your contemporaries still involved. I played with Joe Torre (Yankees' Manager) and roomed with Tony Cloninger (recent Red Sox pitching coach) oh those many years ago. I can't believe that I played my last professional baseball game 42 years ago. My, oh my, where has the time flown?"

Steve's last words of advice to the readers of this book are, "Be vigilant with your health issues, and don't let them sneak up on you, or it may be too late."

As you can see, it was always awfully tough to strike Steve Ryder out. He's still up at bat, and swinging away!

In a nutshell

Steve considers himself the luckiest man alive. He has made the most out of some miraculous medical successes. He enjoys everything about life.

- ✐ Steve had to make many adjustments in his life: from athlete to businessman, and from healthy to medically challenged. Through it all he maintained a positive attitude, which helped him get through it.

- ✐ Despite medical challenges, he continued to be productive in the counseling field and with volunteer activities.

- ✐ Sports had always taken center stage with Steve, and it continues to be a major outlet for him.

- ✐ Steve maintains balance in his life with the continuous help of family and friends.

- ✐ He is passionate about his values and continues to fight for causes in which he believes.

- ✐ Steve has a tremendous will to live and enjoys as much of life as he is physically able to handle. He knows his limitations and works around them.

- ✐ After his heart transplant, Steve maintained an active work, social, and recreational schedule – within reason.

- ✐ Steve advises all of us to be vigilant about healthcare, and not let illness sneak up on you.

9

George Can Do It All

Several years ago I opened my monthly copy of *Boston Magazine*, the chic and hip local publication, and there was a wonderful article about staffing. As I turned the pages, I came upon a full page photo of, you guessed it, our boy, George Rossi, perched atop a gleaming Harley-Davidson motorcycle. He was prominently featured in the article, but his persona of being footloose and fancy free was what the reader walked away with.

He can do it all. He always could. And the irony of it is that he seemed to do it effortlessly. He was looked upon as one of the leading staffing experts in the human resources arena of his time. He was a true icon in one of the toughest businesses around. But we get ahead of ourselves.

George grew up as a tough, street-wise kid from Medford, Massachusetts, a suburb just outside Boston. Hockey was his initial ticket to success, and he was an All-Scholastic out of Medford High School. From there he was one of a few Americans, at that time, to be awarded a full hockey scholarship to Northeastern University, located in the Back Bay section of Boston.

George graduated in 1965 with a degree in Business Administration, concentrating in Finance. He went directly to graduate school, where he received his MBA in Finance. While getting his MBA, he worked as a teaching assistant.

Through hockey and his teaching assistantship, he never had to pay a cent throughout his college career. He also made a ton of contacts through these experiences that would hold him in good stead throughout his professional life.

As he and the other top students in the MBA class were finishing their degrees, they decided to create a brochure promoting themselves, to distribute to Fortune 500 companies. The brochure included an introductory letter from the President of the University. This marketing tactic met with critical success, as they were inundated with inquiries.

George eventually signed on with Honeywell's Corporate Research Center in Minneapolis as a college recruiter. It was not quite in the financial field, but it was in an area that would take him to great heights in the future.

He loved Honeywell, but he and his wife, Maureen, longed to come back home to Boston, so a little more than a year later they permanently moved home. Remember, George can do it all. This time he was hired as the Director of Quality Assurance at the Diamond Crystal Salt Company in Wilmington, Massachusetts. It was a hop, skip and a jump from their Medford roots.

The earthy George Rossi felt right at home in the manufacturing sector of this well-known food manufacturer. He had worked there as a Northeastern Co-op student and knew the people and the process. I don't think George ever looked for a job. His reputation always preceded him. So, barely a year later, the personnel world came calling again. This time, to no one's surprise, Honeywell came after him again. They hired him to work in a local facility at Honeywell's EDP Division in Wellesley, Massachusetts as a Human Resources Manager generalist in Finance, his college major.

A year and one-half later, he was promoted to a Management Development Manager in Waltham, Massachusetts. It was just about that time that Honeywell merged with General Electric, and George found himself on the merger integration task force in 1971. He spent his last year at Honeywell as an Employee Relations Manager for North America.

In 1973, George was recruited by a small, unknown mini-computer company called Digital Equipment Corporation. DEC would go on to become the second (to IBM) largest mini-computer company in the world.

George's first assignment was Finance & Administration Personnel Manager. On September 2, 1975, he became the company's first Director of Staffing. He and his staff (yours truly included) built the acknowledged best world class staffing organization ever assembled. The staff grew to over 300 people. The population of the company grew from 17,800 people in 1975 to over 120,000 people in less than a decade. It was a monumental task given the complexity of the organization.

George had world-wide responsibility. This is where his strengths and talents came into play. He was the out-front guy. He interfaced with the media, with leaders of professional associations, with politicos, and the like. He built a tremendous network of contacts that would help him in future years.

In his early 30s, while his professional life was taking shape, George, who was always a terrific athlete, decided to take up skiing. But George didn't just take up things – he had to excel. So for the last

32 years he has been a skiing instructor at Gunstock Mountain in Gilford, New Hampshire.

He also continued to play in adult hockey leagues, including sneaking out at noon with his buddy, Bill Winslow, for a couple of hours of ice time while they both worked at Honeywell. He also coached at all levels throughout the years. Settling in nearby Winchester, Massachusetts, George spent many years on the town's Personnel Board.

Back to Digital. All was going along well until George had a hand in hiring a new V.P. of Personnel. The V.P. was an Organizational Development guru who was the father of "matrix management." He and George were as opposite as fire and water. George was "Mr. Practical" and the V.P. was "Mr. Theoretical." George eventually moved on to Data General in Southboro, Massachusetts as the Director of North American Staffing.

Data General was quite different from Digital Equipment Corporation and George could never adjust to the differences. After two years, George realized he could gather all of his contacts and networks that he made throughout the years, and move to the third party side of the business to retained search.

It was a natural progression. His initial foray into this world was to open an office for a firm owned by two women out of New York City. The firm was Gilbert Tweed, and with a search in his back pocket from Data General, he opened their New England office out of Burlington, Massachusetts.

He was immediately successful, and after two years, in 1985, was approached by "one of the big boys" at Heidrick & Struggles, a well known search firm with revenue at about $10 million. His success there over the next 17 years is well documented. He had found a home again, similar to Digital Equipment Corporation – a small, high-quality company made up of honest people. George can't deal any other way. Some of his career highlights at H&S include the following:

- Boston Office Manager
- Partner in one and one-half years
- Elected to the Board of Directors
- Carried largest search load
- Conducted all training for newly hired personnel
- Planning committee
- Computer committee
- Executive committee
- World wide responsibility
- Grew offices from 20 to 90 in 17 years
- Grew in revenue from $10 million to $500 million in 17 years

When I asked George why he left, he responded, "The culture of the company changed when we went public. The partnership had more spirit before going public. At the same time, I seemed to lose my fastball. I had inklings of leaving for three years before, but I got to the point where I just didn't want to do it any more. I just didn't want the responsibility of being the largest biller in the office." This was in 2002 – 17 years after joining.

"Also," he said, "my network of contacts were all going out of business (DEC, DG, Prime, Apollo, Wang, etc). I truly didn't have the energy to start building the network all over again."

Regarding retirement, George said, "I made no plans or provisions for retirement. The company going public was basically my pension. I gave them seven months notice, but I was honestly not very effective after I decided to hang them up. My final success was the acquisition of a small search firm named Fenwick Partners.

"The end came in 2002, and I have never looked back. I honestly feel good about what I accomplished. It all culminated in winning the

John D. Erdlen Five-Star Award from the Northeast Human Resources Association in 1997, emblematic of outstanding achievement in the field of Human Resources."

Retirement

"The first thing I had to do," said George, "was get in shape. So, I went back to my original love, hockey. I played morning hockey three to four times a week with a bunch of guys who I'd known for years. Maureen and I have one daughter, Kara. She, her husband, and two daughters live right down the street. And so we took on the role of babysitting a couple of days a week.

"But that just wasn't enough. I went to my place in New Hampshire, looked around, and said, 'This has to be done over.' But I knew nothing about fixing or building. My father had been very handy, but I was all thumbs, so to the library I went. I took out tons of books, talked to lots of people, and became a devotee of the television show, *This Old House*."

Remember, George can do anything he puts his mind to! He began to rip apart the house in New Hampshire. He outfitted the cellar with all kinds of equipment. He had no idea what he was doing, but he was having a ball doing it. He spent three to four days a week, full time, re-habbing the place, including ripping apart rooms – all by himself. "It's a long and lonely process," he said. "It's been a couple of years now and I'm not done yet."

In the meantime, he renovated his daughter's cellar, and built kitchen cabinets for her. "In essence, I've gone from a service career to the world of building things, and I couldn't be happier," he said.

A side hobby to come out of this, was building furniture. "It gives me such a feeling of accomplishment," he said.

His next project might be to add on to the New Hampshire house, or to buy some land and attempt to build a house from scratch. I told you, George can do it all. There is no fear in this 5' 9" dynamo.

Oh, I forgot to tell you about the most recent Winter Olympics in Utah. Yup, George was selected as a volunteer to groom the downhill course for the men's and women's skiing events. His job was to be out there at 4:30 a.m. and make sure the course was ready for competition. He spent two weeks in Utah, where he met some wonderful people and was immersed in the Olympic experience.

Other than refurbishing his old Corvette and riding his motorcycle with his friends, George is just "hanging around." As you can see, George didn't have a retirement plan. But that is how he lived his life. He just did what came naturally. Whatever comes to mind, George does it. That's just who he is.

I asked George, "If you had to do it all over again, would you do anything different?" And in typical Rossi fashion he dropped a bombshell. "Ya, I wouldn't have gone into Human Resources." This from one of the most prominent and successful HR professionals of all time. "I probably would have gone into sales. HR isn't a profession people care about. Over the years I've become skeptical about what the value of HR is to a company. I look at recruitment as separate from total HR. Recruitment is more measurable and you can see the value. That is why I like what I'm doing now. It's like staffing: there is a beginning, middle and end. You can see the results – I built that!

"Retirement has been a definite plus," continued George. "I should have done it ten years ago. I don't want to have anything to do with what I did before! My advice to those getting ready to retire is, Don't over-think it – just go do it! Water seeks its own level. If you aren't lazy, and have some ambition, you can find something to do. Do volunteer work – do whatever, just keep busy, both physically and mentally. I'd advise young people to get other interests, not just work."

I asked George what companies can do to better help their employees as they begin the process of heading toward retirement. He stated, "They could transition into it. When retirement is approaching, start changing their work schedules. If you don't have other interests, and your whole life has been work, you're in big trouble. Companies should give approaching retirees coaching and have other retired people come in to give seminars. This could become a niche industry with all the retirements on the horizon. Call it 'After Work Transition Seminars.' Put your ego aside. You may want to work at a Home Depot or be a starter at a golf course. If you have broad interests, there is no transition. It's amazing how fast the days fly by.

"What do I leave to my lifetime career?" said George. "Well, I would like my legacy to be that I made a difference."

Having personally worked for and with George Rossi, I can attest that he made a huge, positive difference in all the lives he touched. Well done George. Just let George do it – by George!

(Tragically, George was diagnosed with cancer less than a month after this interview. He died two months later. Rest in peace George, rest in peace.)

In a nutshell

George lived life to the fullest. He was totally immersed in everything he did. He completely disassociated from his original occupation overnight. He developed a full-time hobby and never looked back.

- George had virtually no retirement plan. However, his M.O. was seat-of-the-pants for most things.

- Always a free spirit, even in the corporate world, George did what he wanted to do. He marched to his own drummer.

- When he retired, he completely severed ties with his profession, fell in love with re-habbing his property in New Hampshire, and became totally immersed in this project.

- In retirement he went back to his roots. He began playing hockey again in the mornings with his old friends.

- Skiing was always a passionate hobby with George. He continued working as a ski instructor at Gunstock Ski Area.

- He worked as a Downhill Course Groomer for the recent Olympics in Utah.

- In retirement, he recommended putting ego aside, and keeping busy, even if it's working at a Home Depot or as a starter at a golf course.

- He believed if you had broad interests, there is virtually no transition to retirement.

10

A Zest For Life

As I looked for the Somerset Club, I knew I was in for a special treat. There is no indication that this tony Brahmin private club exists behind the doors at 42 Beacon Street. There's no sign on the door – just a street number. "But, how bad could it be?" I thought. It was located a stone's throw from the State House, across the street from the well-known Boston Common, and up the hill from the even more famous television bar, Cheers.

As I entered, I was struck by how quiet it was inside. I was ushered into the Morning Room. The large, heavy leathered furniture was somewhat intimidating, and kind of overwhelming. My mission was to have lunch with Ben Morrill as a prelude to an interview I was writing for my book on retirement.

Despite my initial trepidation, the next couple of hours were as warm, friendly, and fascinating as they could be. Ben Morrill is a charming, nattily attired man of 72, who looks in his 60s and has the energy and enthusiasm of a man in his 40s. He drops names, places, and situations as easily as I drop my fork in a restaurant…but with him it's for real. He was born exactly 300 years after his ancestors came to this side of the pond from England in 1632. He is a 13th generation in America. His ancestor, Justin Smith Morrill (U.S. Senator from Vermont), gave us the Morrill Land Act in 1862 that established the State Universities in America.

The setting was perfect. We were led into the Grand Dining Room where Ben has a regular table in front of a bay window with the backdrop of a beautiful garden. It was fall, and the reds and yellows of the changing leaves framed Ben in a Hallmark Card effect – or at least a Kodak moment.

For the next two hours, during a delightful lunch, Ben regaled us with his stories, which I dare say he has told countless numbers of times. His eyes twinkled as he looked for reactions from his guests. He was in complete control. We were putty in his hands.

We made arrangements to meet for the actual interview, and as I quietly left the Somerset Club, where nobody speaks above a whisper, I opened the door back onto Beacon Street, and was greeted by a splash of bright sunlight, as the people scurried up and down "The Hill." I was thrown back into reality, but was awash in my thoughts of what it would be like when Ben and I went one-on-one to discuss the subject at hand – retirement.

A few weeks later we met for breakfast in the dining room of a Greater Boston suburban hotel. It was here that Ben shared his life's stories and adventures with me. I was not disappointed, for I knew Ben would be a fascinating subject and would fit right into the fabric of this book.

Growing up in the affluent, quaint town of Marblehead on the North Shore, Ben couldn't wait to become an entrepreneur. At 17 years of age, he was already in the commercial fishing business. He owned two lobster boats, worked seven days a week, and was employing a staff.

One of his best friends was Bobby Brown, who stayed in the business after high school, subsequently owned a boat named the *Andrea Gail*, and was the subject of the book and movie, *The Perfect Storm*.

School wasn't first and foremost in Ben's life. He hardly ever cracked a book in high school and was the classic "C" student. One day, he wandered into the admissions office of Boston University's College of Basic Studies (Junior College Division). Ben describes the school as a place for "thugs and under-achievers," although he says that tongue-in-cheek.

Admissions said, "You test okay, and you talk okay, but all you're interested in is how many lobsters you caught in your traps this summer. This is the deal: We'll take you in on probation for one semester." Ben was terrified that he'd flunk out. "Admissions put the fear of GOD in me," he said.

At that time, nobody realized how good Boston University's College of Basic Studies was. Some of the graduates even went on to Harvard and other Ivy League schools. Ben graduated in 1952, and immediately went on to Boston University's School of Communications. At B.U. he was an active participant in the R.O.T.C. program. The Korean War was raging at that time. By tradition, all the male members of his family were in the service of their country. This goes back to the 1600s when his ancestors fought the French and Indians in northern New England.

Graduating in 1954, at 21 years of age, and a newly commissioned second Lieutenant of Infantry, he went for training in Ft. Benning, Georgia. At what Ben called the "Benning School for Boys," he met a friend from back home who had graduated from West Point. This friend, who eventually became a Lieutenant General, talked Ben into going to Jump School. After that it was just natural to go on to Jump Masters School, Aerial Delivery School, and other special schools at Benning.

With all this commitment, Ben added three more years to his military obligation. The five years of active duty found him serving both in Korea and Germany. Unfortunately, he served mostly in a staff capacity which was not to his liking.

But the military quickly realized that Ben had been a communications major in college, and took advantage of his skills. He became a Public Information Officer for the 7th Infantry Division in Korea. After many requests, he was assigned as an Infantry Platoon Leader, Executive Officer, and Company Commander in the 31st Infantry Regiment. "These were some of the best months of my life," he said. "I finally was able to be with the troops and perform in the areas for which I was trained in a great regiment."

Ben completed his service in 1960, and came back to the School of Communications at Boston University as a teaching fellow, and received his Master's Degree. He wrote his thesis on the Military Information System, and how it compared to its civilian counterparts.

His first corporate work experience was with Connecticut General Life Insurance Company (now known as CIGNA). At that time, insurance companies and banks were known for having terrific training programs. The two-year program started Ben off as a management trainee.

Ben had married Priscilla Davis, whose father was a Captain in the U.S. Coast Guard. They lived in the North Shore community of Beverly Farms, and had two children. After the training period, they had two opportunities to move. One was to Roanoke, Virginia, and the other was to Grosse Point, Michigan. They decided they wanted to stay in their home area. In those days, when you turned down two company moves, it was tantamount to ending your career. Hence, Connecticut General asked Ben to leave.

(Tragically, Ben's young wife was killed in an automobile accident on Thanksgiving Day in 1964, leaving him to raise their two young children.)

The next professional move for this enterprising young man was to go out on his own. Ben became an independent insurance broker, primarily setting up small retirement plans called Qualified Pension Trusts for small businesses.

As a successful young agent/broker, he met Attorney Barry Koslow, who was the young Chief Counsel at Union Mutual Insurance Company in Portland, Maine. Koslow was a graduate of Boston Latin High School, Northeastern University, and enrolled first in his class at Boston University Law School. He was a Tax Attorney and an Actuary.

In the new business, Ben became the marketing guy, while Koslow became the inside technical guru. Ben typically put 50,000 miles a year on his car and saw 20 people a week. Morrill, Koslow and Associates moved from qualified to non-qualified pension plans, called SERPs (supplemental executive plans). They would last for 30 successful years setting up these special pension plans.

In 1998 they sold the company to a national company. They had built their business to over 400 clients, mainly banks, hospitals and corporations, with millions in premium revenue.

Ben married Elizabeth Choate in 1967. She was the daughter of Robert B. Choate, who at that time was the publisher of the *Herald Traveler Corporation,* which included two newspapers and television Channel 5 and WHDH. They had a successful and terrific 30 terrific years together. Sadly, Elizabeth died of lung cancer at the same time the business was sold. Ben agreed to remain as a consultant for five years with the new company.

After the untimely death of his wife, Elizabeth, and the sale of MKA in 1998, Ben spent the next five years under contract as a consultant for the new owners, USI Consulting Services. His contract was completed in late 2002, and one would have thought that 70 year-old Morrill would wind down his business affairs and devote more time to enjoying the fruits of his many years of hard work.

Along with everything else that was on his plate, after his wife died, he was given the task of managing the Choate properties held under the family trust. So with all this winding down, the rocking chair on the porch was calling. Whoops! Not just yet. Ben was not through.

He had another idea for an adjunct to the insurance business that had made him so successful. Friends said, "Ben, you don't need the money. Why get into another venture? Why worry at night, get up early in the morning, and work 70 hours a week? Why not sit on your tail, play golf, travel, and fish?" Not Ben! Remember he was an entrepreneur at 17. He had one more arrow in his quiver.

He thought Long Term Care insurance was the emerging market on a retail only basis to individuals. "Why not re-craft the concept as an executive benefit?" he thought. It would give it a different wrinkle. Frankly he never thought of packing it in. It was natural for him to come up with the next great idea and run with it. And so, with a new partner, Jim Latham, the new company, LifeTimeChoice, Inc. was spawned in December of 2002. Today Long Term Care Insurance is heralded to become the most sought after executive benefit of the next decade. The new company is leading the way in this effort.

And 72 year-old Ben Morrill is as giddy and excited about its prospect as he was as a 17 year-old lobster commercial fisherman. He's like a kid in a candy store. So retirement? Not yet – maybe not ever. He says he may build the business up to the point of selling it in ten to 15 years. He'll be in his late 80s then, and who knows what the hot item will be at that time. Whatever it is, you can be sure that Ben will be analyzing it to see whether or not it makes sense for him to get involved.

Now don't think it's all work and no play. Ben is, and has been for many years, an avid sport shooter and fisherman – a real outdoorsman. He was President of the Myopia Hunt Club Skeet Shooting Club, where he is immersed in skeet and trap shooting. He also is a member of the Manchester Yacht Club and the aforementioned Somerset Club of Boston and the Leash Club in New York. He travels annually to South America and to Scotland to pursue his fishing and shooting hobbies.

When asked about preparing for retirement, Ben fumbled for an answer. Retirement really doesn't come into play in his mind. I re-phrased the question and asked him what he thought his legacy might be. What will he leave to the world? What will he be remembered for?

He thought for a while and finally offered these sage musings:

♦ Only 15 percent of the working population really like their jobs.

♦ People who succeed are people who are persistent.

♦ Normally we are only competing against 15 percent of the workforce; the other 85 percent of the people really don't like their jobs.

♦ Anybody can make money, but you only have one reputation.

♦ The harder you work, the luckier you get.

- When you get up in the morning, don't think about retirement. You should have a plan ready before you are faced with the reality of retirement. Whether it's volunteering or taking a course, dammit, do something!

- According to his friend David Barrett, M.D., the CEO of the famed Lahey Clinic, studies are now showing that "People who remain active are less likely to contract Alzheimer's disease or dementia than those who do little or nothing in retirement."

"My legacy? Who knows?" said Ben. "I have 20-plus years to go. No time to think about that."

As I concluded my interview and Ben started to walk away, he turned to me with a glint in his eye and said, "It's as interesting today for me as it was yesterday, and as I daresay it will be tomorrow. Retirement – there's really no such thing in my mind!"

That's Ben, raconteur, bon vivant, all around interesting guy.

 In a nutshell

Ben believes: in things, concepts, people, and in life itself. To this day he is looking around the corner for the next adventure. For Ben, life has been, and continues to be, a series of episodes.

- His positive attitude has enabled him to overcome two personal tragedies. The glass is always half-full, not half-empty with Ben.

- Ben's enthusiasm is infectious, and his charisma engages people.

- His rebellious attitude has been both a positive and a negative influence in his life. He tends to get in trouble – but he loves it. He knows exactly what he is doing.

- Ben is results-oriented. He has an air of confidence that translates to success.

- This dynamo attacks each day as if it was the most important day of his life.

- He has an expansive network of friends and associates. He is the quintessential salesperson.

- Like most of our profiles, Ben keeps physically fit. He looks and acts much younger than his chronological age.

- Ben can't wait to embrace the next great idea. His age and stage of life have no influence on what he will do next.

Part II

Your Money
and
Your Life

Financial,
Health, and
Lifestyle Tips

Financial Tips

It is incumbent upon everyone who intends to retire to be aware of the financial preparation that must be accomplished in order to make a smooth transition. To that end, I have put together a series of tips that hopefully will serve you well as you contemplate the next steps in your life.

1. Unless you are truly an expert in financial matters, engage a professional financial planner early on your road to retirement. By early, I'm suggesting in your 30s.

2. Don't confuse a financial planner with a tax expert. They are two different specialties, and you need expert advice in both areas. A tax consultant, for example, can set up the most tax-advantaged way to pay for your children's and grandchildren's college education, along with getting the biggest bang for your buck in estate tax matters, i.e., inheritance considerations.

3. Be realistic about how much money you are going to need in retirement and what it is going to cost. Inflation and unexpected expenses will invariably eat into your nest egg.

4. Having an accurate and fluid budget is paramount to being financially happy and secure in one's later years.

5. "Your best friend is a dollar in the bank," my mother used to say. Her sage advice is that if you don't have the cash in hand

to buy something, then don't buy it. Her opinions may be somewhat too conservative for my taste, but she is always mindful of the Great Depression. You don't have to take it to that extreme, however, some caution should rub off on you.

6. Having a part-time job in retirement can provide some sanity and a little bit of spending money. It's almost like being a teenager again when your father said, "Get a little job so you can learn to be independent and have your own money to spend."

   The job will also get you out of the house and allow you to interface with other people. It also may provide you with much needed health benefits. Have you cost those out lately?

7. Have your mortgage paid off before you retire so you can minimize your fixed expenses.

8. Remember, you may be retired for 20-30 years, so you need to keep enough assets in stocks to stay ahead of inflation.

9. If you need additional cash flow and you own a home, investigate reverse mortgages, but be aware that fees can be high.

10. Maintain at least three- to six-month's cash reserve so you don't have to liquidate stocks and bonds if a crises arises.

11. Make sure your will is up to date.

12. If you have more than $1 million in assets, discuss bypass trusts with an estate planning attorney.

13. Roll distributions from 401(k) plans into an IRA to maintain tax deferrals.

14. Spend money from taxable accounts first; maintain tax deferred accounts (IRAs, 401(k)s), as long as possible.

15. Remember that you must begin taking withdrawals from 401(k) plans and traditional IRAs at age 70½. Roth IRAs are not subject to this rule.

16. If you begin collecting Social Security at age 62, the monthly amount you receive will be reduced forever.

17. Even if you take Social Security at age 62, Medicare still doesn't start until age 65.

18. Investigate purchasing a long-term care insurance policy. There are differing opinions, so be sure to check them carefully.

19. Consider purchasing an annuity with a portion of your investments to assure that you never outlive your assets.

20. Take advantage of everything you qualify for. For example, if you are a veteran, make sure you utilize all your veteran's benefits. For example, most medications are $7 per prescription. Check with the Veteran's Agent at your city or town hall for eligibility.

21. Review your holdings near year's end. It may be wise to jettison some losing stocks for tax purposes. You may be able to apply the loss of some stocks against capital gains in a given year.

22. Take advantage of pre-refunded municipal bonds. They are relatively safe, you can count on them for income, and they may provide tax advantages.

23. No matter how much money you have, become more conservative with your investing as you get older. If you lose a

great deal of money as you get older, you have less time, and therefore less earning power to be able to recover your losses.

24.   Gifts to grandchildren may be tax-advantageous, as well as giving you a feeling of accomplishment from within.

25.   Start a 529 plan for your grandchildren's college education. It's a win-win for everybody, and can help take some of that enormous financial burden off your children.

26.   You can gift $11,000 per year to anyone without triggering a gift tax. This amount increases to $22,000 when combined with your spouse.

27.   Don't put off financial planning because you are intimidated by the process. It's key that you dive in and get a reality check as soon as practical. The longer you have to set up financial parameters, the smoother the transition will be to retirement or to whatever the next phase will be.

28.   Keep good records. You may want to do an analysis of your last several years of expenses, and if you can computerize your records it may come in handy as you prepare for retirement.

29.   Understand which expenses will remain in retirement and which will fade away. College, mortgage, and fancy cars will all fade away. Health costs, which are probably now being funded from employment, may have to be picked up by you in retirement. This can be a large percentage of your retirement budget.

30.   Project lifestyle changes. Will you need as many nice clothes as when you were working? Will your leisure travel costs

increase? What about those chic restaurants? Can you go to fewer of them? The cost of plays, movies, and gifts all come into consideration. You will have less discretionary income to work with. How do you plan to utilize the existing funds? To prevent running out of money it is suggested that you keep annual spending below 5% of your invested assets.

31. Consider a new car every five years, instead of three.

32. Consider downsizing by moving into a condo and giving up the big house. The savings will come from landscaping, plowing and some repairs. However, condo fees do add up. It's a lot to think about!

33. As you get older, mortgage and college expenses may dissipate. This means you will have more discretionary income to work with, but, *Warning!* Don't fritter this extra money away. This is an opportunity to put the money into a retirement account. Here is where a financial planner can be helpful.

34. Put the maximum amount of money allowable into 401(k) or 403(b) plans. Take advantage of employers' matching funds. This is like free money, and will pay huge dividends in the future.

35. Live within your means. That doesn't mean don't go out, never take trips, don't live!

36. How can I say this gently? *NO CREDIT CARD DEBT!* It's the biggest rip-off in America. Why do you think you keep getting free multiple credit card offers in the mail on a weekly basis? They hate people like me who pay in full every 30 days. I have never paid interest on a credit card.

37. The 2004 Retirement Confidence Survey by the Employee Benefits Research Group found that 50% of workers of all ages have less than $50,000 saved for retirement. Experts recommend that your retirement nest egg, including Social Security, be large enough to provide 65% to 85% of your annual working income for as long as 30 years[1]

38. Over the past 15 years, a great many people have married later in life. This has resulted in having children later in life, which in turn means that college expenses are closing in on you when previous generations would have normally retired. With the tuition of State schools now costing in the high teens, private colleges are approaching the $40,000 a year level. Retirement may have to be put off, or more realistically planning for such a large expense may have to be budgeted over a lifetime. The same premise will hold true for funding weddings.

39. There are many government programs for seniors. Winter fuel assistance benefits range from $400-$500; State programs may cover Medicare Part B up to $1,000; and State law may include property tax exemptions. Food stamps may also come into play for those who qualify.

40. Social Security and working part-time will only supplement your retirement nest egg. Don't think that you can rely on this revenue forever as the core of your retirement finances. It just won't be enough.

41. Here are some quick retirement facts to ponder:

---

[1] Source: Caffrey, Andrew, "Just Subtract The Fear And Add Some Planning," *The Boston Globe*, November 17, 2004, p. J-4.

- ◆ Based upon historical averages, a diversified portfolio of stocks and bonds will earn 6% to 8% annually.

- ◆ At 65 years-old, your investments need to last for 20-30 years.

- ◆ Your expenses will change in retirement, but may not necessarily drop.

- ◆ You must prioritize what is financially important to you.

- ◆ Don't major in avoidance. You must stay on top of your finances, the earlier in life the better.

- ◆ If you plan the financial phase of retirement, everything else will most likely fall into place.

This section should give you plenty of food for thought. It is a menu of suggestions and tips. Not all of them will apply to everyone. However, you should read each one carefully to see whether or not it is applicable to your situation.

Tips for 30-Somethings

It's never too early. Young people, please take note! Your first goal should be saving for retirement. I know this seems backwards since retirement is such a long way off. But, that is exactly why it should be your first goal. When you have time on your side, reaching a goal is easier because of the power of compound interest, which is the concept of earning interest on your interest. Albert Einstein called it, "the greatest mathematical discovery of all time." Each year, interest is earned, not only on what you have saved, but also on what you have previously earned.

When saving for retirement, you should save at least 10% of your income. The best place to save is in a qualified retirement plan such as a 401(k) or 403(b) plan, which allows you to save on a tax-deferred basis. One nice feature of 401(k) and 403(b) plans is that money is automatically deducted from your paycheck, before you have the chance to spend it.

You should save at least as much as the matching contribution your employer makes (usually about 3% of your pay) and then consider switching your savings to a Roth IRA. Roth IRA contributions are invested on an after-tax basis, but the earnings are tax free upon distribution (assuming you are over age 59 and one-half).

Example: Bob earns $50,000 per year and his employer matches 100% of his 401(k) deferrals up to 3% of his pay. Since Bob wants to save 10% of his income, he will save a total of $5,000. Bob should contribute $2,000 to his 401(k) account and $3,000 to a Roth IRA. Since Bob contributed more than 3% of his pay to his 401(k) account, he will get the full match of $1,500 (3% of $50,000) from his employer.

Tip: Always contribute to your 401(k) or 403(b) plan at least to the level of employer matching contributions. It's free money!

Warning: Do not be tempted to take a loan from your qualified plan. You will lose the compounding on the money and pay double taxes on the loan interest since loans are paid back on an after-tax basis.

What the Expert Does: He contributes the maximum amount to his 401(k) plan ($13,000 for 2004, but increasing to $15,000 over the next two years) and also fully funds his Roth IRA ($3,000 for 2004, but increasing to $5,000 over the next five years.)[1]

Saving is the first step, but the savings must be invested. Since you are under age 40, you have many years until retirement. Therefore, your retirement savings should be invested in equities. While stocks are more volatile than other types of investments such as bonds and cash, they have historically provided the highest return over the long term.

The best way to invest in equities is through mutual funds. Mutual funds are pools of money that invest in many different stocks so that one bad stock won't deplete your entire savings. You should further diversify your savings by investing in mutual funds that own different types of stocks. You want to own funds that own large-cap stocks, small-cap stocks, growth stocks, value stocks, and foreign stocks.

---

[1] The maximum allowable contribution for people under age 50 is $4,000 from 2005-2007, and increases to $5,000 in 2008.

On a quarterly basis, you should rebalance your portfolio. That means that you should adjust your account so that you return it to the original allocation levels you chose.

What the Expert Does: He has about 35% of his 401(k) money in large-cap growth funds, 30% in large-cap value funds, 11% in small-cap growth funds, 11% in small-value funds, and 13% in international funds.

Warning: Resist the temptation to time the stock market. Over the short term, the stock market can go up or it can go down. Over the long term, however, the stock market has always gone up (and it has gone up much more than other types of investments such as cash and bonds). No one has ever successfully timed the stock market over the long term. Besides, by investing with each paycheck, you are dollar-cost-averaging, which means you are buying more shares when the market is down and fewer shares when the market is up.

Here's an example:

Purchase Date	$	Share Price	Shares Purchased	Total Shares	Market Value
1/31	100	$ 10	10	10	$ 100
2/28	100	$ 20	5	15	$ 300
3/31	100	$ 10	10	25	$ 250
4/30	100	$ 5	20	45	$ 225
5/31	100	$ 10	10	55	$ 550

As you can see, because of dollar cost averaging, you have a gain of $50 ($550 market value less $500 of purchases) despite the fact that the share price is the same ($10) at both the beginning and the end of the period.

If you continue to save at least 10% of your income each year and properly diversify your investments, you should have a nice nest egg when you reach retirement age. Of course, if you want to retire early, you will need to save more. Many financial websites have calculators that can project your future account balance based upon your age, savings rate, and investment return. For example, try "the ballpark estimate" on the website of the American Savings Education Council (www.asec.org).

As you get closer to retirement, you might want to shift some of your savings to bond mutual funds or money market funds to reduce your risk. Don't forget, however, you might be retired for 20 or 30 years, a period still considered long-term, so you should still maintain a portfolio that contains equities.

You might be wondering how much money you will actually need in retirement. Many experts say you will need at least 70% of your pre-retirement income after you retire. This is just an estimate because everyone's situation is different. If your mortgage is paid off, you may need less than 70%. If you want to do a lot of traveling, or if you have high medical bills, you may need more than 70%. I believe the safest strategy is to shoot for 100% of your pre-retirement income.

When retired, it is important to minimize the percentage of your assets you spend each year so that you don't outlive your assets. To ensure this doesn't happen, you will be safe if you spend 4% of your assets in the first year of retirement and then increase that amount each year by the rate of inflation.

Example: Let's look at Linda. She is 65 years-old and is considering retirement. If she retires at normal retirement age (currently age 64 and four months, but increasing to age 67 for people born after 1959) she can expect to receive about $15,000 per year from Social Security (you can see what you can expect to receive from Social Security by going to their website at www.socialsecurity.gov). That means her investments must generate $35,000 per year. In order to do so, Linda needs a nest egg of $875,000 (4% of $875,000 is $35,000).

What is the future of Social Security? The good news is that Social Security is not going away, even for people under age 40. The bad news is that, given the aging of the American population, people under age 40 are not likely to receive as much as today's retirees (adjusted for inflation, of course). It is a simple matter of demographics.

When Social Security was first instituted by President Roosevelt, the average life expectancy was only around 62 years. Life expectancy today is more than 77 years, and it is continuing to increase. Today, there are three workers for every retiree. By the time people under age 40 retire, there will only be two workers for every retiree.

Remember, Social Security works just like a giant Ponzi scheme. Today's workers are paying for today's retirees. The money being withheld from your paycheck is not going into an account with your name on it. It is being sent to your parents or grandparents.

Sooner or later, however, politicians in Washington will make some changes so that Social Security will still be around when you retire. These changes may include increasing the retirement age, adjusting the factors used to calculate the annual cost of living adjustments, increasing the payroll tax, or instituting partial privatization. The situation with Social Security is another reason you should consider targeting a goal of 100% of your final pre-retirement income rather than only 70%.

Risk

We just talked about the various ways to allocate your retirement account to achieve a diversified portfolio. Why is this important? To reduce risk. There are many types of risks to consider. Outlined below, are a few of the most important ones.

♦ **Market Risk**

This is the type of risk most people think of when investing in equities. It is the risk that you could lose money due to price volatility in the market. As we saw from 2000 to 2003, stock prices can go down. In the long run, however, stocks have returned about 10% per year, so one way to minimize risk is to hold on for the long-term.

We can further minimize market risk by investing in mutual funds, which own hundreds of stocks, rather than investing in individual securities. It is also important to invest in mutual funds whose holdings do not overlap – that is, invest in both growth and value funds, large-cap and small-cap funds, and U.S. funds and international funds.

♦ **Inflation Risk**

This is the risk that the return on your investments won't keep up with the rate of inflation. Many investors, especially after the market decline of 2000 to 2003 are afraid that investing in equities is too risky. What they fail to realize is that by investing in short-term instruments such as money market funds, they are taking on too much inflation risk. Therefore, they may find that when they reach retirement age, their assets have not grown enough to keep up with the higher prices caused by inflation.

♦ **Legislative Risk**

This is the risk that congress will change the rules sometime in the future. As we have little control over legislative risk, it is important that we plan for the worst by ensuring that we save adequately on our own. Also, as we don't know what Congress will do with future tax rates, it is important that we save in different vehicles that are subject to different taxes. Thus, we should save through our 401(k) plans, Roth IRAs, and in taxable accounts.

Health Tips

If you adhere to the axiom, "If you don't have your health you have nothing at all," then this chapter may be the most meaningful of all for you. I have gathered some health suggestions for you to review. Consider the following:

1. Be vigilant about taking care of yourself. Annual checkups after 40 years of age are important.

2. Exercise is extremely important in retirement life. Thirty minutes of physical activity is prescribed on a daily basis. Walking, tennis, and yard work are some of the activities that count.

3. If you don't know what a healthy diet is, seek out a nutritionist.

4. Adequate rest and sleep will prolong life. It all ties together…getting enough sleep, a healthy diet, and proper exercise.

5. Develop hobbies and activities that reduce stress. Try something new that you always wanted to do but never had the time.

6. Keep your mind active and busy. Take courses in ceramics, yoga, or computers, for example. Look for volunteer opportunities in your community.

7. Do a crossword puzzle a day just to keep your mind active and your brain stimulated.

8. Talk to people, be it a friend, family member, or a professional. Don't inhibit feelings that are bothering you.

9. If alone in retirement, be careful not to fall into a depression. Stay busy and have goals and objectives, even if they are miniscule.

10. Cut down on or avoid caffeine all together.

11. Humor is great for your spiritual being.

12. Get dressed and go out every day, even if it is just to the mall. Don't stay in your bathrobe all day.

13. The national Heart, Lung and Blood Institute suggests the following:

    ♦ Avoid nicotine, especially near bedtime and during the night.

    ♦ Don't drink alcohol late in the evening.

    ♦ Don't consume heavy meals close to bedtime, however, a light snack may help you fall asleep.

    ♦ Exercise in the late afternoon to deepen sleep – vigorous exercise within three or four hours of bedtime could inhibit sleep.

14. Attitude is everything as one gets older. A positive attitude goes a long way.

15. Be friendly and you will live longer. Connections with people are so important to your health, that making time for friends should be a priority. An active social network helps you fight feelings of loneliness and isolation.

16. Regular checkups with physicians should be an automatic, and not only with your general practitioner, but also your dentist, ophthalmologist and podiatrist just to name a few.

17. Make sure you do a thorough check of your health insurance options. As you get older, more health problems will invariably arise. It's just a fact of life. Now is the time to ensure that you are more than adequately covered. One catastrophic illness can wipe out a life's savings if not adequately covered. Don't let insurance coverage lapse.

18. Look into Long Term Care insurance. It may or may not be the right thing for you.

There is no reason in today's age why we can't live longer just by practicing good health habits. Following a few simple rules can lead to a healthier, longer and more productive life.

Lifestyle Tips

There are certain lifestyle changes or at least adjustments that have to be made to enjoy your new status in life. I've listed some of them here for your perusal:

1. Have a plan everyday, even if the plan is to "rest" today!

2. Keep a date book and calendar just as if you were still working. Some days the entry will be visiting with friends or going to a doctor's appointment. Other days it could be volunteering or working part-time at the bookstore. Have goals and objectives, even if it is just cleaning out the garage.

3. Check out the local Senior Center or Parks and Recreation events. There is plenty to do, including group day or weekend trips.

4. If you've moved to an over-55 condo complex, the clubhouse is usually a beehive of activity. Card games, bingo, exercise classes, book clubs, trips to the mall or golf courses are just some of the planned activities.

5. Retirement communities are being built so fast they are having a difficult time keeping up with demand. These complexes cater to active, involved seniors who no longer want the responsibility of owning their own home, and believe that downsizing to a condo or townhouse is the way to go. It's a whole new social atmosphere with built in friends, acquaintances, and activities. There is one on the North Shore of Boston that features a billiards room, pub, five restaurants,

a health club, a computer lab, and a swimming pool that is open 24 hours a day. There is even a state-of-the-art television studio where residents can produce and broadcast their own programs.

Many residents are so much busier than they were before retirement, that friends and relatives complain they can never catch them at home.

6. A benefit of this new way of living is that seniors can remain in their home well into their old age, as many facilities offer nursing care on the premises.

7. Some new complexes are expanding their amenities. They offer an on-site medical center, a bank, a hair salon, and a country store and all are connected by indoor walkways. It's certainly the wave of the future.

8. One resident stated that before he and his wife moved to the retirement complex, he would have nothing to do each day except make his wife's lunch. Now he finds it impossible to get bored. All you have to do is show up!

9. On the campus of Lasell College in Newton, Massachusetts, at a four year-old retirement village, residents are required to complete 450 hours of study each year. This program has attracted international attention and has generated a waiting list of over 100. Seniors are going back to college in droves either to revive old passions or explore new interests [1].

10. According to Jenna Russell in a *Boston Globe* article, when Newton's Lasell Village became the first retirement community

[1] Source: Russell, Jenna, "Thirsty For Learning, Seniors Fill College Programs," *The Boston Globe*, November 17, 2004, p. J-5.

in the country to require classroom study, the rule helped resolve an issue of area use by giving an educational purpose to the project. Four years later, under a flexible definition that includes fitness classes and time spent reading and writing, 200 residents average 540 hours of annual study, beyond the 450 required. [2]

11.   In Maine, 6,000 students age 55 and older are enrolled in college programs statewide. Seniors pay a $25 annual membership fee and $25-$50 per class, including books. Programs of this type are sweeping the nation. At the Harvard Extension School, 266 students over the age of 60 are enrolled. World history and religion courses are among the most popular for seniors [3].

12.   In a *Boston Globe* article by Bella English, the message for single seniors is that "dating can be a daunting experience, especially for women. You want someone to talk to, or to go to dinner with. For seniors, dating can be as challenging as rollerblading."

The internet is becoming a popular dating resource, however, one must be careful. You really don't know who is out there. The odds favor men, because it's a simple fact that women have longevity on their side. However, men are looking for women who are 10-15 years younger than they are. Hence, a 70 year-old women is not matching up with a 70 year-old man.

---

[2][3] Source: Russell, Jenna, "Thirsty For Learning, Seniors Fill College Programs," *The Boston Globe*, November 17, 2004, p. J-5.

Dances are popular places for people to meet. Believe it or not, Moseley's-on-the-Charles in Dedham, Massachusetts, which has been in operation for decades, still holds weekly Wednesday ballroom dances, and many Veterans Posts host them on the weekends. [4]

13.   Travel is a great way to spend time in retirement. You now have the time to take leisurely trips without the clock ticking away. Use AAA or some service to plan your itinerary. RVs are popular with seniors, and elder hostels are an inexpensive way to go. Line up some friends and family to visit along the way to not only to break up the trip, but to reconnect with people whom you haven't seen in years. Cruising is still the most popular leisure time trip activity with retirees.

14.   Senior retirees are terrific workers. They have flexible work schedules, and always show up on time. Their work ethic is a throwback to the '50s and '60s. This is a win-win for both the employer and the senior citizen. It's just enough hours to help out with spending money, and satisfies limited obligations for the employer.

15.   There are a myriad of volunteer activities. All you have to do is look for them and put yourself in play. A few suggestions may be:

  ♦ reading to elementary school children

  ♦ town government committees

  ♦ peopling crises hotlines

---

[4] Source: English, Bella, "Starting All Over At 70 Something," *The Boston Globe*, November 17, 2004, p. J-8.

- youth athletics coaching
- hospital customer service desks
- babysitting for grandchildren

16. In a recent *U.S. News* article, Betsy Streisand relates seven secrets of successful retirement. They are as follows:

    - Don't Call it Retirement
      Re-hirement or free-tirement are two of the many new buzzwords coined to describe the third stage of life.

      Save Earlier, Save Smarter, Save More
      One-third of the baby boomers have virtually nothing saved for retirement. Putting something away now and contributing regularly, even seemingly trivial amounts, will pay big dividends later.

    - Get a Life…Plan
      Since daily activities are so tied to the quality of life, failing to have a game plan can be devastating.

      Build Your Human Capital
      Invest in your education, skills, and other human capital by returning to school, volunteering, and making contacts in your field before you retire. As you get older, it will be vital to be good at what you do, and keep your skills current.

    - Increase Your Social Security
      The relationships people have with their families and friends will sustain them in their later years. Surveys suggest many retirees spend more time enjoying their adult children and grandchildren than they do on any other activity.

- **Stop Getting Older**
  Exercise, eat better, lose weight. If one message about aging has become loud and clear it's that fitness and health consciousness can go a long way. Studies also show that simply spending more time around younger people can work like a B-12 shot to renew your energy, stimulate your mind, and keep you feeling young.

- **Prepare for the Worst**
  Even though we think we will live forever, and we are more fit than previous generations, health challenges may crop up. Long-term care insurance is a relatively new phenomenon that should be explored. On average, a nursing home stay is about $4,000 a month, and can easily wipe out a life's savings in a short period of time. Take the time to check out all the options. [5]

If you choose, retirement can be a golden time in your life. It's up to you! You are no longer bound by restrictions that may have plagued you most of your life. It's time to think outside the box. Don't think of it as God's waiting room; just think of it as the next phase of your life. Appreciate what you have. Look at life as if the glass is half-full – not half-empty. Take advantage of the openness and freedom that you are allowed at this stage of your life. Enjoy the sunsets, the friendships, and count your blessings!

---

[5] Source: Streisand, Betsy, "The Seven Secrets Of Successful Retirement," *U.S. News* Special Edition, June 2004, p. 5-8.

Conclusion

When we began our journey, the burning question, after reaching the traditional retirement phase of our life was, after the euphoria of the first 90 days, what are we going to do to fill up our time every day?

My goal was to take you through the work, and subsequent next phases of ten very diversified backgrounds. Reading between the lines these profiled retirees had both similar and dissimilar traits. Let's take a look back and see if there was a thread running through their stories.

Most of the people profiled had been quite active in their heyday. They were very involved. As a matter of fact, a great many were Type-A personalities, who were either somewhat rebellious or certainly very strong-willed. They were all high achievers. They came from different backgrounds, races, and genders. Entrepreneurial, risk-takers, highly disciplined achievers, multi-task oriented, fitness fanatics, curious sorts, and successful, are just some of the adjectives and action phrases that come to mind as I flip through the lives of those profiled.

Let me stress that there is no right or wrong way to approach the challenge of retirement. For some people, sitting on the rocker and taking time to reflect on memories of the past may be the ticket to happiness. However, statistics prove that too much of this can be detrimental to both your physical and mental well-being. Conversely, being as active as you were during your work-a-day years could be construed as no retirement at all. Hence, there probably should be a balance or happy medium between these two theories.

I have shown by profiling these fascinating individuals, that there are a myriad of activities to choose from. If you couldn't get a full plate out of our ten friends, I gave you several more tips and options in the second part of the book. The financial, health and lifestyle tips should cover most of the contingencies that you will be faced with.

This has been quite a personal challenge for me. As you will recall, one of my retirement goals was to attempt to do something I had never done before. That was writing a book. This project has truly been a labor of love. I thoroughly enjoyed each and every phase, and never dreamed the process could be so complicated. Working with my mentor, Martha R. A. Fields, and her associate, Jessie Shea, has made the whole process much easier. They have guided me all the way. I thank them for their wise counsel.

Pauline Kelly took my words and thoughts and sculptured them into the flowing pages that make up this book. Her talent is displayed by her creative cover design and typesetting that was presented to you, the reader. But most of all, her friendship and counsel during some of the rough times made her invaluable to the success of this book.

I do hope that you have enjoyed this book, and that I have removed the mystique of what to do during the next phase of your life. Do whatever you believe is right at the time, but don't be afraid to adjust the routine as need be. Just make sure you....*Get Off Your Rocker Before You Go Off Your Rocker!*

Bibliography

Bach, David. *The Automatic Millionaire.* New York: Broadway Books, 2004.

Bolles, Richard Nelson. *What Color is Your Parachute?* Berkeley, CA: Ten Speed Press, 1991.

Caffrey, Andrew. "Just Subtract the Fear and Add Some Planning," *The Boston Globe*, November 17, 2004, p. J-4.

English, Bella. "Starting All Over at 70 Something," *The Boston Globe*, November 17, 2004, p. J-8.

Gray, Barbara E., with Cleveland, Debra Regan. *A Woman's Ways & Means,* Framingham, MA: Drummer Cove Publications, 2002.

Perls, Dr. Tom; Silver, Dr. Margery H.; with Lauerman, John. *Living to 100: Lessons in Living to Your Maximum Potential.* New York: Basic Books, 1999.

Pond, Jonathan. *Your Money Matters*, New York: G.P. Putnam's Sons, 1999.

Russell, Jenna. "Thirsty For Learning, Seniors Fill College Programs," *The Boston Globe*, November 17, 2004, p. J-5.

Streisand, Betsy. "The Seven Secrets of Successful Retirement," *U.S. News* Special Edition, June 2004, p. 5-8.

Swedroe, Larry E. *Rational Investing in Irrational Times.* New York: St. Martin's Press, 2002.

About the Author

Barry Bograd has always been a curious sort of guy. An entrepreneurial risk taker, he has been involved in many different worlds from owning race horses, to coaching Varsity High School Football, to hosting many long-running cable television shows, to being active in town politics, to owning a multi-million dollar consulting business. Human Resources was his main profession for 40 years, but music, sports, politics, his family, and just being fascinated with people have been other passions throughout his life. He has traveled in uncharted waters and has a problem saying no. Living in his retirement years with his wife, Elaine, in Framingham, Massachusetts and Moultonborough, New Hampshire (overlooking Lake Winnepesaukee) inspired him to take on the challenge of writing his first book. The project has been a labor of love. Barry hopes that you take away some great ideas from this guide to retirement and that it gives you the impetus to *Get Off Your Rocker Before You Go Off Your Rocker!*

Printed in the United States
29467LVS00005B/388-489

9 780976 881209